Motorhome and RV Retirement Living

Motorhome and RV Retirement Living

*The Most Enjoyable and Least Expensive
Way to Retire*

Jerry Minchey

Stony River Media

Minchey, Jerry. Motorhome and RV Retirement Living: the most enjoyable and least expensive way to retire / Jerry Minchey

ISBN 10: 098449684X
ISBN 13: 978-0-9844968-4-6

1. Recreational vehicle living.
2. Retirement.
3. Retirement, Places of.

Published by Stony River Media
Asheville, North Carolina
StonyRiverMedia.com

Dedicated to Henry Minshew, who is still driving his 38-foot Class A motorhome up and down the east coast at the age of 92. Uncle Henry recently told me, "I know I probably shouldn't be driving, but I love to get out on the road and go places."

Contents

Introduction

"I live in a a very small house, but my window looks out on a very large world."

~ Henry David Thoreau

This book is not intended to tell you everything there is to know about RVs. It's not meant to try to convince you to retire and live full time in an RV.

This book is meant to give you the unbiased information you need to decide for yourself if living full time in an RV is the lifestyle you want for your retirement.

By the way, the terms RV and motorhome are used interchangeably by most people. That's why I include both words in the title of the book. I will generally use the term RV throughout this book to describe both the towable and the drivable type of RVs. Sometimes I will use the term motorhome just to be different.

The appeal and dream of living an RV lifestyle has not changed much since the first RVs were introduced back about 1910. Freedom, adventure, fun, and relaxing are words RV owners frequently use to describe why they enjoy the RV lifestyle.

To me, living full time in an RV is a way to live a low-stress, simplified life and it has the extra benefit of being very inexpensive. I also find that being part of a community of people who want to do things and go places keeps me feeling young and keeps me moving. One friend recently said, "I didn't want to wait until the aches, pains and stiff joints made it too hard for me to climb in and out of an RV, so I decided to hit the road now while I still can."

When you ask people what they would like to do when they retire, many of them say that they would like to travel. But conventional travel consisting of airplanes, hotels, motels, car rentals, restaurants, etc., can quickly deplete a nest egg. On top of that, it's tiring and stressful.

Compare that to the simplified, low-cost and relaxing lifestyle of living full time in an RV—and sleeping in your own bed while you travel. If this lifestyle intrigues you, keep reading.

To start with I want to dispel the myth that living full time in an RV is just for the wealthy. Yes, you can spend some big bucks on some of the fancy, top-of-the line motorhomes, but you can also buy a nice used RV in the $10,000 to $20,000 range or less. I'll get into more on RV prices later in the book.

Is the RV lifestyle the right choice for you?

If you want to keep your same 4-bedroom brick house with two new cars in the driveway and belong to the same country club, maybe you need to keep working. A lot of people enjoy that life and want to hold onto it for as long as possible.

But if you're ready for something different, let's look at some options. First of all, living full time in an RV is not necessarily better or worse than how you're living now—it's just different. It's different in a fun, exciting and adventuresome way. It's a lifestyle many people love, but it's not for everyone.

Many people, as they approach retirement, look forward to traveling, having freedom, enjoying adventure and being around other people who are doing interesting things. In other words they don't want a boring life. They want to experience something different.

And of course, they want to do all of this well within their budget. That's one of the biggest advantages of living full time in an RV—and the RV lifestyle really is one of the least expensive ways to live. I'll explain that more later in the book.

I'm sure you have a lot of questions and that there are many things you want to know about the cost and what's involved in this lifestyle. A lot of this book is about retiring on a much lower budget than most people think about when they think about living full time in an RV.

I will mainly be talking about used RVs in the $5,000 to $50,000 range. I know that's a wide range and yes, you can find nice RVs in the $5,000 to $10,000 range, but many people end up buying something in the $20,000 to $40,000 range for retirement. Of course, if your budget will allow it, you can find some really luxurious RVs when you look in the $100,000 and $200,000 range. I highly recommend that you don't buy a new RV as your first RV. I will go into the reasons why later in the book.

Living full time in an RV may be ideal for you and it may not. Making your decision on whether you want to live full time in an RV (and which type of RV) gets easier the more information you have access to. Consider your decision making process and your RV selection process as an adventure and enjoy the journey.

While living full time in an RV, I have experienced much more excitement and adventure than I ever imagined when I set out on this lifestyle. To me the freedom and flexibility are the best parts. On top of that, it's very relaxing, low-stress and inexpensive.

I also love being around the like-minded and interesting people I meet. I have more friends now than I ever had in my previous lifestyle. I find that I have a lot in common with my new friends. The things I had in common with my previous friends were that we worked together or lived near each other or attended the same church, but not so much because we had any or many common interests. I still stay in touch with many of my former friends and maybe even more so than before–just not face to face.

Some people make things happen. Some people watch things happen and some people wonder what happened. I think you'll find that the people you meet in campgrounds are the ones who make things happen. After all, if they had not made decisions and made things happen, they wouldn't be in a campground living in an RV.

I think the whole full-time RV experience is summed up by the title of the Christmas classic movie with James Stewart, "It's a Wonderful Life."

Let's get started.

Chapter 1

Living Full Time in a Motorhome/RV

Dare to live the life you have dreamed for yourself. Go forward and make your dreams come true.

~ Ralph Waldo Emerson

I now live full time in a 2002, 34-foot Class A National Sea Breeze motorhome. On the next page is a picture of my 'home.' This picture was made when I pulled into a Cracker Barrel restaurant for lunch recently.

I tow a 2012 Prius using a dolly (because a Prius, like a lot of cars, can't be towed with all four wheels on

the road). I'll talk more about towing a car in a later chapter.

Living full time in an RV takes some getting use to. Not long after I began living full time in my RV, I was getting ready to take a trip. I got my suitcase out and started packing it and deciding what I would need to take on the trip. Then it dawned on me. I don't need to pack a suitcase. Everything I own is going with me. All my life I had packed a suitcase when I took a trip. It takes time to break a habit. Of course, I still pack a suitcase (or a backpack) when I take a trip in my car.

When you live full time in an RV, you're not on a permanent vacation. And you're not a tourist every-where you go—you're a temporary resident. You're not camping for a weekend. It's the way you live. When I visit friends I've had them tell me that they're going to fix me a home-cooked meal. I really appreciate it, but I eat home-cooked meals all the time—meals that I cook myself. I don't just snack. I have a full kitchen and I have every appliance and cooking utensil in my RV that I had in my stick and brick home.

There are between 250,000 and 7 million people living full time in RVs (depending on how you define full time and which experts you listen to). For example, there are a lot of people who live in an RV full time—part of the time. They live in their RV during the winter or during the summer. Are these people full-timers? It depends on your definition of the term "full time."

Anyway, let's just say that there are a lot of people who live the RV lifestyle. For a high percentage of them, it's their only home.

You don't drive every day

The average RV is driven about 3,500 miles a year. That's less than 300 miles a month. That's why if you look at a 10-year-old RV, it will likely have about 30,000 to 40,000 miles on it.

Even if you have a goal to visit every state or see every national park, make your first year slow. Don't overdo the travel. The states and national parks will all be there next year and the year after. They're not going anywhere. Slow down and have fun. Enjoy the journey.

A lot of people think of living in an RV as traveling all the time. Some people do that, but most people stay at one campground for several days or even a few weeks—sometimes for months. As the next picture shows, some people stay in one place long enough to have a garden.

Well, maybe not really. If you look closely, you may be able to see that the plants are all in pots. When the garden owners are traveling, the pots can be placed inside the RV until they get to the next campground. The plants get plenty of light in the RV, so traveling doesn't even slow down their growing process.

Pros, cons, and things to consider when you're thinking about living full time in an RV

The Pros:

- Freedom. You can live where you want to and move with the seasons. You are not tied down. You can change your mind tonight and live somewhere else tomorrow night. You can go wherever whim and chance might take you.

- One of the things I like even more than going to different places is the freedom to know that I can go if I want to.

- If you change your mind about the RV lifestyle, you can sell an RV in a matter of weeks instead of the months or years it can take to sell a house.

- If you don't like your neighbors, you can move to another location in a matter of minutes. You can do international travel and not have to still be paying living expenses back home while you're gone. Just put your RV in storage at $50 a month or so while you're gone.

- You can even get reduced insurance rates when you're not driving your RV and have it in storage.

- When I was between houses, condos and RVs, I spent six months in Costa Rica. It was a fun and interesting experience. It was inexpensive, but it wouldn't have been if I had been paying for rent (or a mortgage payment), electricity, cable TV, Internet, taxes, etc., back home. When you're living in an RV, you have this freedom to almost totally eliminate expenses back home while you travel abroad. Whether you ever do it or not doesn't matter. Just having the freedom to do it is a good feeling.

- Having everything I need handy is one thing I really like. I know where all of my tools are, my books, my clothes, etc. Nothing is in storage or somewhere out in the garage or somewhere up in the attic. It's all right here.

The Cons:

I had a hard time finding things to list in this section because I like almost everything about RV living—but that's just me. Here are some things that may be considered cons for some people:

- You don't have as much privacy in campgrounds (sometimes you do, but not always).

- Sometimes there are noises like barking dogs, RVs pulling in and out, being located next to busy highways, railroad tracks, etc.

- You won't have your 'back-home' friends nearby to enjoy and spend time with.

- Your grandkids may not be close by and if they come to visit you in the summer, it can get crowded after a short time. Of course, they would probably enjoy it—at least for a while. It would be an adventure for them. For example, where you are this summer is different from where you were last summer.

- Your regular doctors may not be close.

Other Things to Consider:

- If you have a partner, do you both really want to do it?

- Do you both have hobbies, interests or things you really like to do that don't involve the other person—reading, writing, knitting, crafts, computers, golf, fishing, hiking, painting, etc.?

- Do you have things or people 'back home' that you need to look after or take care of—rental property, aging parents, etc.?

- Headsets or ear buds are mandatory when two people are living in an RV.

- How comfortable are you and your spouse being together 24/7? The little things that annoy you about your spouse can get magnified when you're together 24/7 in a small space. Most people need a little time apart. There are ways to do this while living in an RV, but give it some consideration. Be sure to schedule some "me" time.

- Just like in a stick and brick home, there will be unexpected maintenance expenses from time to time. Allow for these expenses in your budget.

- If you act like a tourist and want to eat out a lot and see and do things like a tourist, you will end up spending money like a tourist. To keep your expenses low, you have to remember that you're not on vacation.

- Life in an RV can be much less expensive than living a traditional stick and brick lifestyle—but you have to learn a few secrets and techniques that I will cover in later chapters.

To get a feel of what it's like to live full time in a motorhome or RV, visit the website *RV.net/forum* and check out the Discussion Forums.

Another very useful website is Chris and Cherie's site at *TechNomadia.com.*

As you will see from Chris and Cherie's website, the RV landscape is changing. Technology is now allowing non-retired people to live the RV lifestyle. You will see a lot more people in their 30s, 40s and 50s in campgrounds now than you did just a few years ago. This is because they can now use the Internet and technology to work and earn a living while on the road.

Becky Schade is a 30-year-old, college educated, single female living full time in her RV. She does workamping (which will be described later) more than she uses technology to fund her travels. You can read her articles and learn more about what she does and how she lives her life by going to her web site at *interstellarorchard.com*

You can also check out Howard and Linda's website, *RV-Dreams.com.* The site has a lot of informative articles and it has an active Discussion Forum as well.

You will find all four of these websites very informative and useful. Take time to check them out and you will have a much better feel for what it's like living full time in an RV.

RVers are a diverse bunch. There are doctors, lawyers, school teachers and Indian chiefs living the RV lifestyle, but you may not know that when you meet them because in the RV culture no one asks you what you use to do. They just ask, where have you been, where are you going, what interesting things have you seen, etc.

Even though I talk a lot about spouses and couples in this book, you will see a lot of solo RVers in your travels. There are more solo women than men it seems like. There are several websites where solo RVers share concerns, stories, etc.

More on what it's like living full time in an RV

The cost of living full time in an RV can be substantially less than living the traditional lifestyle in a brick and stick house.

You have the option to not travel for a month or so. Stay in a campground where you get free camping in exchange for some volunteer work, and your living expenses will be almost nothing—except food, insurance, etc.

One woman told me, "You will also save a lot of money by not buying things you don't need. Going shopping will no longer be considered a form of entertainment. There's no place to put things you don't really need." How many pairs of shoes do you really need? I had not thought about it, but she's right. I don't buy 'stuff' like I used to.

One good way to learn more about what it would be like living full time in an RV is to talk to people who are doing it. If you don't know anyone personally, the next best thing is to watch some interviews where people who are living full time in RVs are talking about their experiences.

I've put some links to videos I think you will find interesting on LifeRV.com.

As you will see in these videos, some people are living on a frugal budget and some are living on a higher budget. Some people are working part time and some are not. These videos are about seven or ten minutes long. They were created by Chris and Cherie and hosted on their website that I mentioned earlier, *Tech-Nomadia.com*, and you can find a lot of other useful information on their website.

Look around while you're there. Here are some of their videos that I think you will find interesting and informative. I've put direct links to the most interesting videos on the resource page at **LifeRV.com/book**, including:

- Tales from Nomads: What's Newell
- Tales from Nomads: Co Bear
- Tales from Nomads: Mutiny
- Tales from Nomads: Our Odyssey
- Tales from Nomads: Geeks on Tour
- Tales from Nomads: Interstellar Orchard

What do I miss about my old lifestyle?

A lot of non-RVers ask me this question, but I can't think of much I miss about my previous lifestyle. I think more about what I would miss if I gave up my RV lifestyle. Here are some of the things I would miss if I gave up living in my RV:

- Being free to travel and see the country
- Going to music festivals and rallies
- 75 and 80 degree January and February days
- Hour-long coffee times with friends
- Spending time with wonderful, like-minded friends
- Sunrises and sunsets over water
- Never having to deal with snow and cold weather

- Always having friends nearby to have a glass of wine with from time to time without having to take more than a few steps

- Sitting around a campfire with interesting friends

- Being able to explore charming little towns

- In other words, total freedom

When I talk to other RVers, I find out that for most of them, their biggest regret is that they didn't embark on the this lifestyle sooner.

Make your decision

The information in this book along with the links, references and other books I recommend will give you the information you need to make your decision—but you have to make the decision.

I remember sitting in a marketing class at Harvard one time and the instructor asked a student what he would do in a case we were studying. The student said that he would go out and get more information. That was the wrong answer.

The instructor said, "Every decision you make for the rest of your life will be made with incomplete information." He said, "Make a decision and if it's wrong, you can change it." He said that businesses lose more money by not making a decision than they ever lose by making the wrong decision.

I think that concept applies to personal decisions too.

What if you change your mind about RVing?

Full-time RVing is not for everyone. Not everyone is cut out for this lifestyle, individually or as a couple.

Selling an RV can be done fairly easy in a matter of a week or two or a month or two at most. In fact, you can list your RV on eBay and sell it in three days—and at a fair price.

You are not locked in. You can change your lifestyle in a heartbeat. And if you do your homework and find a great deal (and do a good job of negotiating) when you buy your RV, you can likely sell it for more than you paid for it.

Bottom line: Do a reasonable amount of research, soul-searching and fact finding and then make your decision. You will never have all of the information, but remember, when you're living the RV lifestyle, it's very easy to change your mind, sell your RV and live a different lifestyle.

Keep reading and then make your decision

Chapter 2

Can I Afford the RV Lifestyle?

It's nice to get out of the rat race, but you have to learn to get along with less cheese

~ *Gene Perret*

When someone asks me how much does it cost to live full-time in a motorhome, I tell them it's like asking how much does it cost to live full-time in a stick and brick house or an apartment. It cost whatever you have. You can live extravagant or frugal. In a nut-shell, the RV lifestyle can be a lot less expensive than what most people are spending to live the way they're living now.

Most people go about thinking about being able to afford retirement backwards. They wonder, "How much money will I need for retirement?"

People ask, "Should I retire or keep working?" The answer is simple. Consider the life you have now. How much do you like it or hate it? Compare that to the life you would have if you retire now. A lot of people think, "I'm making good money and if I retire, that income will stop."

The problem is that they are spending most of that money as fast as it comes in. They're not saving much of it. In other words, it takes the amount of money they're making to support the lifestyle they're living.

Obviously, you will have less income if you retire now than you would have if you keep working, but are you spending it as fast as you're making it? Maybe you've already retired and most of your income has stopped, but your living expenses have not changed much.

Which lifestyle will make you happier—your present lifestyle or the RV lifestyle?

Also, keep in mind that there's no guarantee that both of you will still have your health and be able to enjoy the RV lifestyle a few years from now. You may want to consider doing it now while you still can. You can sit in a rocking chair later.

These are decisions that only you can make. For a lot of people, work is their life. They're good at what they do and people look up to them. They feel important on the job. It gives them a purpose in life and they actually enjoy working—sometimes way more than they think. Other people hate every minute at work.

Sit down and add up your retirement income. How much will be coming in each month from Social Security? How much from any pension or investments you have? How much cash (or things that can be converted into cash) do you have—your home, your investments, etc.? What you have is what you have and it's not likely to change much.

With this information you can decide what kind of retirement you can afford—and sustain. After you read this book and look at the numbers, you will most likely realize that it will come down to deciding *if* you want to live the RV lifestyle and not whether you can afford it.

You're on this earth and you have to live somewhere. **Living full time in an RV is one of the least expensive options you'll find.** Of course, there are some very nice RVs that will cost you a fortune, but you can live in a much, much lower priced RV and be just as happy—well, almost as happy.

It's the lifestyle that's enjoyable and will make you happy—not the price of the RV you live in.

Of course, you'll have the initial expense of buying an RV. I have two whole chapters later that will help you decide what kind of rig you should get, how much it will cost and how to get the best deal, but here is a quick overview.

Typical costs for a good used motorhome will run between $10,000 and $50,000. Of course, you can go a little less or a lot higher than this. Don't spend a lot on your first RV. After you live in one for a while, you'll have a better idea of which of the many RV options will work best for you and there are a lot of options.

You can spend a lot more than $50,000 on a used RV. Many of the late model, nicer RVs can easily run well over $100,000 and used diesel rigs can run much higher.

The diesel engines will run well over a million miles and the Ford V-10 gasoline engine (which is now used in all gasoline RVs) will easily go 200,000 to 300,000 miles with no problem.

With either engine, you will wear out everything in the RV way before you'll have any trouble with the engine. In fact, be leery of a used RV with very low mileage. Not being driven for months or years at a time can cause a lot of maintenance problems for an RV.

One big difference between living in an RV and living in a typical neighborhood is that in a typical neighborhood, most people buy a house that's as expensive as they can afford (or sometimes a little more expensive than they can afford). That's not the case in the world of RVs.

I know of a case where a couple had over half a million dollars in the bank and they were living in a $5,000 RV.

Many people decide that when they retire, they don't need or want a big expensive house or RV. It's not a status symbol like it was when they were in the rat race. They don't have a lot of company and they find that they're happier with one of the less expensive RVs.

Other costs associated with living full time in an RV

The fee for campsites can be a major expense and can vary from quite high to very reasonable—or even to zero when you're boondocking. Boondocking is a term used to describe camping where it's free, but where there is no water, electricity or sewer hookups. We'll talk more about boondocking in a later chapter.

Here are some typical numbers to think about. Campsite fees range from about $18 a night to $45, with $20 to $30 being about typical for a single night.

Another option is to book a camping space for a month or more at at time. You can stay in some very nice campgrounds for $300 to $450 a month. This includes electricity, WiFi, water, sewer, trash pickup and sometimes cable TV is included. Monthly rates run about two times the weekly rate, so whether you stay for two weeks or for a month, the cost will be about the same. Also, by staying a month you get to relax, meet people, see the sights, and enjoy what the local area has to offer.

There are ways to get discounts. For example, if you join *PassPortAmerica.com* for $45 a year, you can stay in thousands of participating campsites for half price. As you might expect, some conditions apply. You can join *Escapees.com* and get discounts too.

To cut expenses while they're traveling, a common practice of RVers is to stay in a campsite for about $24 for one night and then stop and boondock two nights in Walmart parking lots along their way. That means that they spent a total of $24 for three nights of camping or $8 a night. Of course, if you stay three nights in Walmart parking lots and one night in a campground, you will get the average price down to $6 a night. Not all Walmarts will allow you to park overnight, but most will. Be sure to check with the manager and get permission before you spend the night.

If you're traveling and just making miles, stopping at Walmart parking lots two or three nights in a row and then getting up and hitting the road again each morning is a great way to cover a lot of miles with minimum campground fees.

Also, since you're not putting down leveling jacks, extending the slide-outs, hooking up water, electric, and sewer, there's nothing to do the next morning except start your engine and hit the road. But be sure to crank your TV antenna down if you cranked it up the night before. One easy way to remember to do this is to hang your ignition key on the antenna crank handle.

What about the cost of gasoline or diesel fuel?

Everyone thinks that the cost of fuel is a major expense with an RV and it is if you travel almost every day or travel back and forth across the country—and some people do.

But if you stay in one campground for a month and then travel 300 miles to another one, this would add up to 3,600 miles a year. As we discussed earlier, this is about average for most people who are full-time RVers.

Let's do the math. Assume that you drive 3,600 miles a year and are getting nine miles per gallon. Some RVs get 8 mpg or less and some get 10 mpg or more. How fast you drive and what kind of rig you have will affect your mileage, but these numbers are in the ballpark.

That would mean that you would use 400 gallons of gas a year and at $3.50 a gallon, that would be $1,400 a year for gas or $117 a month. You're probably spending more than $117 a month on gas now in your present lifestyle. What if you drive 7,000 miles a year, nearly twice the national average? That's still only $234 a month for gas.

As you can see from the above analysis, the cost of gas is not really an issue. It comes down to which lifestyle you would enjoy the most—the RV lifestyle or your conventional stick and brick lifestyle.

By doing a little research you will be better informed and able to recognize a good deal when you start physically looking at RVs. Keep in mind that there will be some maintenance expenses with any RV. Most of the time it will be nothing major. The engines run forever. You will need new tires every five to seven years.

By the way, when looking at tires, you can't go by the tread. You will have to go by the date code (which I will explain in a later chapter). Almost all motorhomes will have tires with good treads.

With your stick and brick house you will have maintenance expenses, such as $5,000 for a new roof, $6,000 for a new heat pump or air conditioner, etc. Your RV probably won't have maintenance expenses that high, but do budget $1,000 or so a year depending on the age of your rig, how much you travel and, of course, a diesel (also called a DP for diesel pusher), will be more expensive to maintain. A lot of the things you spend money on will not be something that has to be done—at least, not immediately—things like new carpet, reupholstering the couch, etc.

One of the things that make the RVing lifestyle so affordable is that you have a lot of control over how much you spend each month and you can change it in a heartbeat. When you live the conventional lifestyle, you don't have many options to change your monthly living expenses.

For example, if you have expensive repair work that needs done on your rig this month, you can almost totally eliminate fuel cost, by not traveling. You can also almost (if not entirely) eliminate camping fees by boondocking on public lands, in Walmart parking lots (only one or two nights at a time) or by doing some volunteer work at a state or national park campground in exchange for free camping. You can also do what is called workamping for a month or so and get free camping.

You can find out more about workamping at *WorKamping.com* and I will talk more about it in the chapter on, "Ways to Make Money Without a Computer." In a nutshell, workamping is where you get free camping in exchange for working a few hours a week. Sometimes there is a small salary paid also.

Bottom line: You can buy your first RV very inexpensively. Trade up later if you want to when you know more about what you want. When you get to the chapter about "How Much Will an RV Cost?", you will see just how much RV you can get for very little money.

Your monthly living expenses (assuming you are not paying off debt or making payments on a car or RV) can vary from less than $1,000 to over $3,000 a month depending on how much you travel, how much you eat out, and other personal and entertainment expenses you choose to make. This amount includes campsite rental with water, electricity, sewer, WiFi, and cable TV.

It also includes food, insurance, an allowance for some maintenance, and some gas. You can get this amount even lower by boondocking some and/or doing volunteer work in exchange for free camping.

Of course, you can spend a lot more.

Bottom line: I think after reading this chapter you will agree that, "Yes, you can afford to live full time in your RV." Now let's go on and look at some more information to help you decide if living the RV lifestyle is what you want to do.

Chapter 3

What Kind of Rig Should I Get?

With an RV you can enjoy wine and roses on a bread and water budget.

~ Author Unknown

There are several different types of RVs for you to consider. The book I recommend in the Other Resources chapter, *Buying a Used Motorhome - How to get the most for your money and not get burned* by Bill Myers, does a great a job of describing each type of RV and the pros and cons of each, so I will only briefly go into the subject here.

One thing to keep in mind is that all RVs have issues and problems. Even if the one you bought didn't have anything wrong with it when you bought it, going 60 mph down the rough Interstates (I-95 up and down the East Coast comes to mind), your RV will take a beating worst than a house being in a magnitude 6 earthquake and it will need some repairs from time to time.

The more people spend on their RV, the more upset they get when something goes wrong. I guess that's human nature. Spending a lot of money when buying an RV doesn't guarantee that things won't go wrong.

Most of the things that go wrong with RVs are not expensive to repair (and a lot of the repairs you can do yourself), but there are things you have to deal with and they can get frustrating if you let them. Accept the fact that RVs will have issues (a polite way of saying—problems). Deal with the problems and get on with your journey.

How the different RV classes got their names

Before I go into describing each type of RV, let me clear up the mystery about what seems to be a nonconventional way of naming RVs.

The first motorhomes were called Class C because they were built on a chassis. Then they came out with the big (Greyhound bus style) rigs and since these were bigger and fancier, they were naturally called Class A.

The next type that came along was the smaller type of motorhome that was a little bigger than a van and the only class left was the Class B. After all, they didn't want to call them Class D RVs. That would imply that they were inferior. So as Paul Harvey used to say, "Now you know the rest of the story," about how RVs got their names.

The five basic options you have when choosing an RV:

- **Class C:** This is probably the most common type of RV you see on the road. It has an extension over the cab and looks like a U-Haul moving truck. It's fairly easy to drive and depending on the size, it gets about 9 mpg. It has a reasonable amount of storage, but not a lot.

- **Class B:** These are the ones that look like an oversize van except that they are taller. They drive almost like an SUV. They are easy to drive. They get 15 to 17 mpg and are a good way to go if you plan on doing a lot of traveling. But since they're so small, they are not a good choice if you plan to live in them full time. Also, they have very little storage room. They are way too small for two people to live in full time. The other disadvantage of Class B motorhomes is that they're expensive. Used ones are expensive mainly because they get good gas mileage and they're easy to drive and a lot of people want them—it's supply and demand.

Some of the more expensive Class B models have a slide-out to give you more room inside—but they're still too small for full time living, in my opinion.

- **Camper/Trailer:** These come in all sizes from very tiny to as big as some Class A models. Of course, the bigger they are, the harder they are to maneuver and backing a trailer takes some practice and experience. Also, the bigger the trailer, the bigger the truck it takes to pull it. Many of them have slide-outs that make them very roomy. Two of the biggest disadvantages are that it's not nearly as easy to pull one as it is to drive the motorhome type rigs and they are a lot harder to get set up when you stop. And if you get a big trailer, it will take an expensive truck to pull it. If you're not going to travel much, a camper trailer can be a good choice. And a lot of men like to have a pickup truck whether they need it or not—with a trailer type camper, they will need a truck.

- **Fifth-Wheel:** These are RVs (recreational vehicles), but they're not motorhomes because they don't have a motor. These RVs have an overhang in the front (called a gooseneck) and it connects to the large swivel type hitch that's inside the bed of a large pickup truck (that's where the name "fifth-wheel" comes from). They can be even bigger than a big Class C RV. Most of them have a bedroom in the front and one in the back, which provides privacy for each bedroom. They have a lot of room and are a good choice if you're traveling with kids. They're easier to pull and they have more room than a camper/trailer, but they are more expensive and can require a larger truck to pull them than what is required to pull a trailer type camper. Keep in mind that with a fifth-wheel, you have the option of spending most of your budget on the camper and then buying a used (maybe even a very used) truck to pull it with. If you're not going to be traveling much, that's a good option. Of course, you can do the opposite as well. Keep in mind that the truck to pull a large fifth-wheel could cost more than the RV.

- **Class A:** This is the type of RV that looks like a Greyhound bus. The older models made before 2000 generally didn't have slide-outs, but most of the ones made after 2000 have anywhere from one to four slide-outs. They have a lot of room, are easier to drive than a fifth-wheel or a camper/trailer rig. They get about 7 to 9 mpg and have a ton of storage inside and underneath in the storage bins that are usually referred to as the basement (I guess because the storage bins are under the main living area). The best part is that they're generally less expensive (used ones, that is) than a large Class C, Class B or a fifth-wheel (including the truck it takes to pull it).

New Class A RVs are expensive, but there are

some real bargains out there in the used market. New ones are expensive because they're expensive to build, but they depreciate rapidly. The reason used ones are such a good buy is because a lot of people think they can't drive the big Class A rigs and most people think that they don't get good gas mileage. Both of these assumptions are wrong. With a little practice, they're easy to drive (see the next chapter about driving a motorhome). They're a lot easier to back than a trailer or a fifth-wheel. They back just like a car—they're just a little longer. Also, contrary to popular belief, the gas mileage is maybe one mpg less than a Class C. The reason is that Class A RVs are very aerodynamic and a Class C with the overhang over the cab is a very non-aerodynamic vehicle.

Which type of RV is the best choice for full-time retirement living?

The Class A, B, and C motorhomes are all easier to drive (and much easier to back) than a fifth-wheel or trailer, but that doesn't answer the real question. Let's dig into the subject a little more.

The answer to the question about which type of RV is best for your situation, needs and wants will depend on a lot of factors, such as, how much you plan to drive, how much space you want, your budget, etc.

I've seen people living full time in Class Cs, in trailers, and even a few in Class Bs, but most people who retire and live full time in their RV, go with either a used Class A or a used fifth-wheel. I went with a used Class A.

Some people like the large fifth-wheel RVs and you can get some really good size camper/trailers. Even some Class C RVs are quite roomy. I recommend that you look at several floor plans and see which ones seem like home to you and consider how much storage space each type has and how much you'll need. This information and first-hand inspections will help you decide.

One advantage of a fifth-wheel is that you don't have to buy and tow a car. Just park it, unhook it and you have a vehicle. Of course, it will be a gas-hog compared to most little toads (the car that's being towed), but if you don't plan to be driving much, that wouldn't be a big issue. As you can see, there are a lot of things to consider and there's no one best answer. I'll talk about towing a car in a later chapter.

From what I've seen in the RV parks about 40% of the full-timers have Class A rigs, about 40% have fifth-wheel rigs and maybe about 20% of full-timers have trailers or Class C RVs. I don't mean that this is the ratio of the different types of RVs that you will see on the road or in campgrounds; I'm talking only about the RVs that people who live in them full time have.

Keep in mind that you probably won't get an unbiased answer if you ask other RV owners whether you should get a Class A or a fifth-wheel. People usually like what they have. If they didn't, they would sell it and buy something different. The prices are about the same when you consider the truck required to pull a fifth-wheel.

One of the things I love about a Class A RV is the big front windshield. It's a great way to see the country when you're driving. And when you're parked, it's like having a picture window. Of course, there are curtains so you can close off the windows at night.

The basic information in this book will generally apply to all types of RVs, but I'm sure you will notice that it is slanted towards the Class A motorhomes since that's what I think most people will be happiest with if they're going to retire and live full time in an RV. The extra storage that you have in a Class A is very useful when you're living in your RV full time.

Remember, you don't have to pick the perfect RV or even the perfect type of RV for your needs and wants. That's because after going through the rest of this book, you'll be equipped to find and negotiate a great deal on an RV and then if you change your mind and decide that you want a different type of RV, you'll be able to sell the one you have within a week or so and make a profit on it.

As my father always said, "You make your money when you buy something—not when you sell it." You usually sell something for about what it's worth, but you can buy things for less than they're worth if you do a little searching and negotiating.

I have a friend who usually sells his RV and buys a different RV one or two times a year and he almost always makes a profit when he sells his RV. By the way, the best way to sell an RV within a week or so and at a fair price is on CraigsList or on eBay.

Constantly changing RVs doesn't appeal to me. I like the idea of keeping an RV for a long time. I know where everything is and how to fix most things on my RV now. If I had a different one, I would have to learn all of that all over again.

For example, recently I blew a fuse when I was hooking up the lights on my tow dolly. I checked every fuse in the two fuse boxes and couldn't find the blown fuse. Then I got on one of the RV discussion forums (*RV.net/forum*) and asked if anyone knew where the fuse was for the towing lights on the rig I had.

I found out that there was a 3rd fuse box out front under the hood and when I located that fuse box and opened it, the first fuse I checked was the blown one. If I get a different RV, I will probably have to hunt for fuse boxes again. By the way, most RV owner's manuals are not very detailed or complete. I think I will keep the RV I have for a while.

Your first RV should not be a new one

If you buy a new RV, you will be stuck with it for several years unless you're willing to take a big loss. That's because new RVs depreciate even faster than new cars.

After you've lived in your RV for a while, you may decide that you want a different type of RV or you may even decide that you don't like the RV lifestyle. If you buy a new RV, you will never be able to sell it and get anywhere near what you paid for it.

Also, most new RVs have a strong chemical smell for a year or even several years. Some people are very sensitive to the smells and fumes that are out-gassed in new RVs.

I was at an RV show in Atlanta and, like everyone else, I was walking through the high-priced RVs and drooling. I was in one that looked ok, but it didn't seem overly fancy like some I had been in. This one had a $300,000 price tag on it. I couldn't see what was so special about it and then I saw a sign saying that it was built with all old and seasoned materials. There was absolutely no detectable smell.

Of course, you could buy an older used RV for $30,000 or less and it wouldn't have any smell either.

After you have lived in an RV for a year or longer, and you're sure you know exactly what type you want, buying a new one that you plan on keeping for years, might be a good option, but by all means, your first RV should not be a new one—period.

Of course, since you're giving a lot of thought to what type of RV you want before you buy your first RV, you may find out later that you bought just the right RV and one that you really love.

One last point about buying a new RV—we all know that one of the advantages of buying a new car is that at least for a while, you won't have any maintenance problems.

That's not the case with a new RV. They all have issues. Everybody in the RV world will tell you that you should never buy a new RV and head out on a long trip. There will always be things that will need to be fixed. These things will most likely be covered under warranty, but your dealer can't take care of them if you're halfway across the country.

Bottom line: Most people who live full-time in their RV choose either a fifth-wheel or a Class A. (A few people do choose a Class C.) Look at several floor plans, but since you bought this book to get my opinion, my opinion is to go with a Class A for full-time living, unless you can find a strong reason why you want a fifth-wheel or other type of RV.

A Class A rig is much easier to drive (even when you're pulling a toad). I'll talk about towing a car in a later chapter.

A Class A is also easier to set up when you stop for the night and easier to get back on the road when you're ready to take off the next morning.

In fact, if you pull into a campground and it's raining, you can push a button and let the leveling jacks down, push a button and let the slides out and then you can sit back in the recliner and have a glass of wine and watch TV. You never have to step outside in the rain. You have full power for everything and if you need more power, you can push a button and start the generator. Do you get the idea that I like a Class A?

Chapter 4

Can I Drive an RV?

The best time to start thinking about your retirement is before your boss does.

~ Author Unknown

Sure, I could drive it if everybody else would stay off of the road and I could straddle the center line and drive down the middle of the road. That's what it feels like the first time you get behind the wheel of a big Class A RV. If you're pulling a fifth-wheel rig behind a big truck, it's the same feeling.

To convince you that you can drive any type of RV—including the big Class A models, let me explain it this way. It would be a lot easier to learn to drive a Class

A or fifth-wheel RV than it would be to learn to drive a car if you had never driven one.

Another way to look at it is that it would be easier to learn to drive an RV than it would be to learn how to ride a bicycle if you had never ridden a bicycle. When you consider these two facts, I think you can understand why I say it's easy to learn to drive an RV.

The good news about Class A RVs being perceived as hard to drive is that it keeps the price down. A lot of people automatically go with the smaller Class C RVs for that very reason. This runs the price up on Class C RVs. The fact is that a used Class A RV (for any given year and condition) in many cases is less expensive than a Class C. And of course, you get a larger and more functional living space in a Class A RV than you do in a Class C. You also get more storage space inside and you get a ton more storage space in the outside storage bins with a Class A.

You can save a lot of money if you will get over the notion that you can't drive a Class A rig. Let everyone else keep thinking that they're hard to drive. As long as most of the world thinks that, the prices will stay low.

In a nutshell, here's how to drive an RV

One approach to learning how to drive an RV is to just get in and start driving and hope that you and the RV both survive until you learn how to drive it. I think a lot of people use this approach, but there's a better way.

This chapter is not intended to make you an expert RV driver just by reading it, but my intentions are to cover enough driving instructions to convince you that you can become a great RV driver.

When you first start driving your RV, it will feel like you're driving a battleship. You will feel like you're taking up all of your lane and half of the opposing lane.

While you're driving, glance at the four or six mirrors (two or three on each side) and make sure that you can see the painted line on the highway on both sides of your lane. This will let you know that you are where you need to be even though it sure doesn't feel like you are. After a little while driving, it will become second nature and your sub-conscious mind will take over and driving down the road will finally feel normal.

Keep in mind that everyone has a tendency to crowd the right side of the road. This is ok when you're meeting a big truck on a two lane road, but for normal driving just keep it equally between the center line and the edge of the road line. The person in the co-pilot seat will feel like you are way too far to the right and the co-pilot will feel like you're going way too fast.

To me when I'm in the right seat it looks like I'm about straddle the white line on the edge of the road—but when I look in the side mirror, I see that the rig is right inside the edge of the road line where it should be.

How to turn to the right

The front wheels on most Class A rigs turn 50 degrees, so a good rule of thumb to remember when making right hand turns is to pull forward far enough so that your hips are just past the curb, sign post or whatever it is you want to miss. Then turn as sharp as you can to the right. Of course, glance at the sign post or curb that you want to miss while making the turn.

Also, on right-hand turns watch the back, left corner of your rig. The back part that's behind the rear tires will swing out to the left. Watch and make sure your back end doesn't swing over and hit a car in the lane beside you. And if you're pulling out of a camping space, make sure your back end doesn't swing out and hit the RV beside you.

When you're making a turn at an intersection, if you find that you can't make the turn without going over in the oncoming lane, just stop and wait for the traffic to clear and then go on over in the lane and on your merry way. You probably won't receive the RV driver of the year award (at least, not from the people having to wait behind you), but you will never see them again anyway, so it doesn't matter. Don't try to back up and *never* back up if you're pulling a toad.

How to turn to the left

When you're turning left, you have a lot more room and you can make a wide turn with no problem. Be sure to pull forward and make a reasonably sharp turn. Don't make a haphazard turn and let the back left corner of your RV go over and hit the car waiting at the intersection for you to make your turn.

Walmart can help you learn to drive

One of the best ways to learn to drive your RV is to spend an hour or so in a Walmart parking lot early on a Sunday morning when it's almost empty. Get off in a corner by yourself. Set up some empty cardboard boxes and practice making turns. Notice how the back end swings out wider than the back wheels when you make a sharp turn. It's easy to forget about the back end swinging around.

When you're in the Walmart parking lot, line your RV up so that the edge of the coach is even with one of the painted stripes that mark a parking space. Have your co-pilot stand outside as you make a sharp turn. Have them mark how wide the back of your RV swings past the parking space line. This is your over-swing.

Knowing this distance can prevent you from causing costly damage to your RV and to other vehicles. When you do this exercise and actually see what happens, it makes the concept of over-swing more real than just reading about it.

How much space do you need to make a turn? Have someone stand six feet in front of your RV. Then slowly make a sharp turn. You should just miss them. Have them note how much you missed them by or how far they had to back up to avoid being hit.

Knowing all of these measurements will make you a good and safe driver. Most RV drivers don't actually know this information about their rigs. They just wing it.

Backing your RV

Some people tell me that they think they could drive an RV, but they're not sure about being able to back it into those camping spaces. You can back into tight spaces blindfolded — you really can, because all you have to do is listen to the person directing you. You turn right when you are told to (or signaled to turn) and you turn left when you are told to.

One other important thing is that you also stop when you are told to. Backing an RV is a lot easier than backing a trailer. When you turn the steering wheel to the right, the back of the RV goes to the right and vice versa. What could be easier? Of course, you have to turn the steering wheel in the opposite direction you want the back end to go when backing a fifth-wheel or trailer.

I have six mirrors and a backup camera to watch what's going on behind me, but I trust the person standing behind the rig more.

In other words, don't worry about backing. You can do it like a pro. Just watch for the hand signals in your mirrors and listen to what your lookout person is telling you. The backup camera has a microphone and the sound comes in loud and clear through the rear view monitor system.

And as an extra precaution, the rear view camera has a grid superimposed on the color screen showing you what's 3 ft., 2 ft., 1 ft. and then zero feet behind you.

While you're in the Walmart parking lot, take the time to practice backing. Use your cardboard boxes and assume that they are other RVs or power poles. Most of the time when you're backing, you will have someone guiding you. An important point is that if you can't see the person who is guiding you, STOP. Don't keep backing and assume that everything is all right. Try backing with someone helping you and then while you're at it, try backing all by yourself just using your backup camera and mirrors.

If you don't have a co-pilot, there are always other RVers available to help you, but proceed with caution. I was at a campground one time and a guy was backing into a camping spot. A woman was guiding him and the top corner of his RV rubbed against a big tree limb. Luckly, there was no major damage. The woman said, "I wasn't watching that side." Duh?

The backup camera is your plan B to make sure you don't back into a post or big rock. With a little experience, you should be able to back into a spot by yourself by using the mirrors and the backup camera, but I always like to have someone back there saying, "'mon-back" and then "stop" as my plan A.

More points about driving

Go over speed bumps very slowly and if at all possible, go over them straight on so that both front tires hit them at the same time. If you go over them at an angle, you're going to get four bumps instead of two and the resulting twisting of your RV could cause glasses in the cabinet to tumble out into the floor and maybe even cause seams in the roof to crack. This could cause leaks. Maybe I'm exaggerating, but you get the idea.

Measure the height of your RV from the pavement to the highest point (usually the top of the air conditioners). You will be OK going under Interstate highway overpasses, but be careful on back-road overpasses, tunnels, and especially at service stations.

Nothing beats the experience of just driving down the Interstate to get the feel of driving your RV. The more you drive it, the more comfortable you will feel doing it and who knows, one day you might just receive the RV driver of the year award (if there is such a thing).

One other thing to keep in mind is that after you've done all of this practice and spent some time driving your rig and now you feel comfortable and confident driving, don't be surprised if you feel a little uncomfortable again when you get behind the wheel the next time—especially if it's been a week or two since you drove it the last time. The good news is that it's like riding a bicycle—your driving skills and confidence will quickly come back to you.

Of course, you don't want too much confidence. Back before I got my pilot's license, my flight instructor told me one time that I had more confidence than skill. That's a bad thing for an airplane pilot. Now that I have over 2,500 hours of flying under my belt and have an instrument rating, hopefully I have the skill to go with my confidence.

The key to driving your RV is to drive slow and often until you get the feel of driving the big rig. If you're driving a Class C RV, all of the above information will apply, but it won't be as pronounced or as hard to get used to. You should still spend time in the

Walmart parking lot doing all of the maneuvers and measurements discussed above.

An RV driving course manual

There's a good RV driving course manual available for $30 at *RvBasicTraining.com*. I own this book and I highly recommend it. If you're going to spend $30,000 to buy an RV, spend another $30 and learn how to drive it.

This is a 46-page manual, but there are a lot of pictures and drawings included in the 46 pages, so it's not that much actual reading. If you read this manual and do a few of the parking lot exercises, you will know more about how to drive an RV than most of the drivers on the road.

Sign up for an RV driving course

Of course, the ideal thing to do is to sign up for an RV driving class. Search Google for the phrase, "RV driving class" or "RV driving school" and you will find when and where there is a class being held in your area.

The classes usually run a full day with part of the time in a classroom and part of the time with you actually driving your RV. The costs typically run about $300 to $500 for the day.

As one friend of mine put it, when you're in a Class A RV, you're sitting up high and even if someone hits you broadside, you probably wouldn't be hurt and your rig is covered by insurance, so don't worry. Just go enjoy the journey. I don't know if I like his way of thinking, but I guess it's true.

Licensing

You don't need a special license to drive a motorhome in most cases. Generally if your RV is less than 40 feet long and weighs less than 26,000 pounds, no special license is required. To check the requirements in your state take a look at this website: *Changingears.com/rv-sec-state-rv-license.shtml*

Plan ahead

One last point. To be a good RV driver you need to think and plan ahead. Don't pull into places you can't get out of. Remember, you can't back an RV if you're pulling a toad. When pulling into or out of a service station, restaurant, etc., go slow, watch all corners of your RV and by all means watchout for your overhead clearance. If it even looks close, stop and get out and look or have someone get out and look.

Bottom line: Yes, you can quickly learn to drive your RV like a pro by following the above advice and with a little practice. You will soon be able to thread a needle (so to speak) with your RV (whether you're going forward or backwards). Don't decide not to enjoy the RV lifestyle just because you're afraid that you can't drive the thing.

Chapter 5

How Much Will an RV Cost?

The question isn't at what age to retire, it's at what income.

~ George Foreman

The first thing everyone wants to know when considering whether to live the RV lifestyle or not is, how much will it cost?

The real answer is that it's within your budget. How do I know that? Because it's within almost anyone's budget. Since you've bought this book and are considering it, I'm sure you can afford it because it can be so much less expensive than most people think.

If you're even remotely thinking about living full-time (or even part-time) in a motorhome, by all means buy Bill Myers' book that I referenced in Chapter 3. I don't mean to say the same thing over and over, but download the book for $2.99 and it will save you a lot of money when you buy your RV.

Find a link and information on *Buying a Used Motorhome—how to get the most for your money and not get burned* at *LifeRV.com/book.*

Start your search on eBay

The fastest way to get an idea of what RVs are selling for is to check out eBay. Be sure to look at the "Completed listings" to see what RVs actually sold for. Sometimes the starting bid or the reserve price is way out of line and the RV will not sell.

To see the "Completed listings" and learn the actual prices RVs sold for, log into your eBay account and then in the top right corner of your screen in small print (just to the right of the big blue "Search" box) you will see the word, "Advanced." Click on this link and then enter the keyword, "motorhome." Scroll down and click on the Completed listings box and below that enter a price range or at least, enter a minimum price. If you don't enter a minimum price, you will see 20,000 items including mirrors, clocks, headlights and everything that has the word, "motorhome" in the listing.

Then click on the blue "Search" box. This will take you to the list of completed auctions. The prices shown in green are the ones that sold and the prices shown in red are the ones that didn't sell because their reserve price was higher than the highest bid or else they didn't get a bid because their starting bid was too high.

I think you will be pleasantly surprised at how little some of these motorhomes sell for.

Websites that show prices for used motorhomes:

- *motorhomerv.com*

- *rvtrader.com*

- *nadaguides.com/RVs* - NADA Pricing Guide

- *kkb.com* Kelly Blue - Book prices

- *CampingWorld.com/rvsales*

The above websites generally show you the fair market going-rate retail prices of motorhomes, but these are not usually the real bargains. There are other websites that show prices for RVs. These are just some examples.

In addition to looking at eBay to find the bargains, checkout CraigsList at *Craiglist.org*. Note that this website uses the "dot org" and not the normal "dot com" suffix.

The more you investigate, the less you have to invest

In addition to checking CraigsList and local RV dealers in your area, keep in mind that you can find some good bargains outside of your area. Check Florida, Arizona, Texas and New Mexico. A lot of people go there to retire and then when they pass away or go into an assisted living arrangement, their children sell their RV. The children don't know what it's worth. They just want to get rid of it. There are some real bargains to be found in these areas if you're diligent.

Also, spend some time looking at used RVs on the lots at some local RV dealers. This way you can see a lot of different types of RVs and see several floor plans with very little effort. And yes, you can sometimes find some really good deals on used RVs when buying through a dealer.

Of course, make sure the RV has not been sitting unused for a year or so. Sitting unused is one of the worse things that can happen to an RV. You could have a lot of maintenance problems if you buy an RV that has not been used in a long time.

You can hire a local RV mechanic in the area where the RV you're interested in is located to do an inspection for you. If they find something major wrong with an RV, this could save you from making a big mistake. Most of the time even if everything is in reasonably good condition, they can usually find enough minor things that you can negotiate with the seller to fix and almost always more than offset the cost of the inspection.

Also, if you don't want to go get the RV yourself and drive it back to your location, there are companies that will bring it to you for a reasonable fee. So don't overlook searching for RVs outside your local area.

RV prices are more negotiable than auto prices

Some people don't like to negotiate, but in the RV market almost all prices are negotiable and not just a little bit, but big time negotiable. You can save a lot of money by doing just a little bit of negotiating. Use the simple negotiating techniques described below and you should be able to get your RV at a great price. For new RVs it's not uncommon to get a dealer to drop the price by 20% to 30% or more. Don't expect dealers to drop the price that much on a used RV, but I have seen private sellers drop their prices by that much.

Note that not a single one of the following statements says that you won't pay the price being asked. You imply it, but you don't actually say it. You are always free to accept the price that the seller is asking.

Here are my 7 all-time favorite negotiating phrases for people who don't like to negotiate

1. **ALWAYS, ALWAYS flinch at the first price or proposal**
   You should almost fall out of your chair because you are so shocked. Do this even if the price you hear is way less than what you expected. Flinch and say, "That's WAY out of my budget and then shut up. Don't say a word. Just sit and wait for the price to drop.

2. **Next, when you get the lower price quote, you should say, "You've got to do better that that."**
   And then again, you shut up. If you open your mouth, you won't get the next price concession. If you say yes to the first offer, the other person will know that they quoted you a price that was too low. They may even try to find a way to increase the price. They may say something like, "Well let me see if the boss will go along with this price" or, "Let me make sure that this is ok with my wife."

3. **If you make a counter offer ALWAYS Ask For a Much Lower Price Than You Expect to Get.**
   One of the cardinal rules of negotiating is that you should ask the other side for more than you expect to get. Henry Kissinger went so far as to say, "Effectiveness at the negotiating table depends upon overstating one's demands."

4. **Never offer to Split the Difference**

   It's human nature to want to "play fair." Our sense of fair play dictates to us that if both sides give equally, then that's fair. Realize that the other side is almost always willing to split the difference, so you should try to get a little better deal than that.

5. **How to use two powerful negotiating techniques all in one sentence. The two techniques are: "Absent higher authority" and "If I could, would you."**

   We've all experienced the "Absent higher authority" technique. For example, "Our insurance regulations won't let you go back in the shop" or "The loan committee wouldn't go along with those terms."

   You don't get to talk to the loan committee (it doesn't exist) and you don't get to talk to the insurance company. It's a higher authority that you can't talk to.

   Here's how to use the technique in your favor for once.

   When you're down to the final negotiations, you can say, "If I could get my (financial adviser, spouse, or some absent higher authority) to go along with this, would you replace the carpet?

   Notice in this statement that you haven't agreed to anything.

   The owner or salesperson is in a position of feeling that they need to go along with what you're proposing to keep the deal from falling apart.

6. **Nibble for More at the End**

   You can usually get a little bit more even after you have basically agreed on everything — if you will use a technique I call nibbling.

   You can say, "You ARE going to have the carpets professionally cleaned, aren't you?" or "You are going to replace the windshield wiper blades aren't you?"

   The sales person is already thinking about what he is going to do with his commission. The last thing he wants is for this sale to fall through. He will usually give just a little more if you "nibble."

7. When you're getting close to the end of the negotiations and everything is just about nailed down, **say, "I'm getting nervous about this" and then SHUT UP**. The other party will think the deal is about to fall apart and they will likely throw in one more concession to seal the deal.

Bottom line: Use some or all of the above negotiating techniques and you can easily cut the price you end up paying for your RV by thousands of dollars.

Chapter 6

Pitfalls to Avoid & Buyer Checklist

If water is too clear, it will not contain fish; people who are too cautious will never gain wisdom.

~ Author Unknown

When it comes to buying an RV, I have three guidelines I recommend that you follow:

1. There are some things that should be considered deal killers. I recommend that you walk away fast if you find any of these things. (I will list what I consider to be deal killers later in this chapter.)

2. Go with your gut. If a deal seems too good to be true or the deal just doesn't feel right or you don't have a good feeling about the owner or sales agent, walk away.

3. There are a lot of great RV bargains on the market right now and in this market as a buyer with cash (or the ability to get financing), you are in the driver's seat. Think about RVs when you remember the old country song, "There's More Pretty Girls than One."

By the way, if you don't feel confident to fully inspect the RV you're considering buying, you can say that the deal is subject to having your mechanic inspect the RV and verify that everything is in good condition and is as represented. After it has been inspected, if there is anything new that you learn, you can usually get the owner to fix the problem or else lower the price a little to allow you to get it fixed.

Below is my list of the things you need to be sure to check off before you buy an RV. These are things that you should be able to take a look at yourself. Note that not everything has to pass, but if it doesn't, and you buy the RV, you want it to be because you considered a fault or problem and decided that you could fix it or that it wasn't important to you. What you don't want to happen is to find out after you buy the RV that there was something that you forgot to check.

Make pictures and keep good notes as you do your searching. After you look at a few RVs, the details will all start running together. Don't depend on your memory unless you are only looking at a very few RVs.

After you have checked everything on the list and made a note of anything that is a problem, then you can decide to ask the owner to fix the problems or you can decide that it's not a big deal. And of course, you can use the problem items in your negotiating to get the price down.

Here's my Buyer Checklist:

There are seven things that I consider to be deal killers for me. You might be a little more tolerant on a few of the items than I would be, but personally, I don't want to deal with these problems right off the bat when I buy an RV.

Armed with this checklist, you are ready to start your search. Enjoy the adventure.

1. **Mildew**—This is especially important to look for when buying an RV in Florida. It may not be much of a problem in Arizona, but in Florida it can be. Mildew can be almost impossible to get rid of, particularly when it's back inside the walls. It's also very bad for your health. You don't have to see it. If you can smell it when you first walk in, it's there. Walk away. Be sure to check when you first walk in. Your nose will adjust to it quickly

and you won't know it's there after a minute or two, so be observant when you first walk in.

2. **Has the RV been smoked in**—For some people this is not a big deal, but for me it's a major concern and a deal killer. Be sure to consider this when you first walk in. Like mildew, you won't be able to detect it after your nose has adjusted to the smell. By the way, if you don't think your nose will block out smells quickly, try this. Blindfold someone and then hold half of an orange, lemon or onion near their nose and ask them to identify the smell. They can almost always do this easily. Hold it there and ask them to tell you when you take it away. In a very short time, they will usually say that you have taken it away. That's how fast your nose disregards strong smells. I guess it's nature's way of saying that if there's a strong smell and you can't do anything about it, you might as well ignore it.

3. **Water damage**—This can be expensive to repair and there may be a lot more damage than is first visible. Look for discoloration or stains on the ceiling. Look for stains around the windows and on the carpet around the walls and in the corners.

4. **Soft or spongy places in the floor**—This could be a sign of water damage also. Be sure to check around the commode and in the kitchen.

5. **Signs of mice**—Look around where the water pipe comes into the RV. Look for signs of mice inside the kitchen cabinets. Mice can do a lot of damage and getting rid of them can be hard and you can end up with a bad smell for a long time when you use poison to kill mice. Just walk away.

6. **The owner doesn't have a clear title**—A motorhome is considered to be a vehicle just like a car. It has a VIN (Vehicle Identification Number) and a title. You have to pay the annual personal property tax and put a new license plate sticker on it every year. If there is a small lien on a higher priced motorhome, I might consider it, but for lower priced motorhomes, it's not worth the hassle.

7. **If I catch the owner (or agent) not being truthful with me**—If he will lie about one thing, he will lie about more things. I like to ask a few questions that I already know the answer to in order to see if he is truthful.

   For example, when I was looking to buy the RV I live in now, I was looking at an RV that had almost new tires on it. I asked the salesman how much a new set of six tires costs and he said $4,000 to $5,000 or more. (He was inflating the price of the tires to show me what a good deal I was getting by buying this RV.) RV tires are expensive, but not that expensive. $2,000 to

$2,500 will buy a good set of tires. I didn't buy that RV because I no longer believed anything the salesman told me.

Not deal killers, but other things you should check to make sure they work

- Generator (Check to see that it cranks relatively easy and that it puts out the proper voltage under load with two air conditioners running.)

- Leveling jacks

- Awnings

- Water heater

- Microwave

- Refrigerator (on propane and electric)

- Slide-outs

- Furnace

- Air Conditioner (check both if it has two)

- Check the date-code on the tires

  Look for the 4-digit date code on the tires (sometimes it's on the inside and you may have to crawl under the RV to see it). It's the last four digits in the series of numbers and letters that start with "DOT" as shown in the photo below. The first two digits are the week and the second two are the year the tire was manufactured. The tire in the photo below was made in the 3rd week of 2013. Tires are only good for five to seven years. (After five to seven years tires will dry rot and start to crack and become dangerous to drive on regardless of how much tread is left.)

Bottom line: Don't depend on your memory. Make a list of the things I've described above and especially the seven deal killer items. Make sure you check these things off as being inspected for each RV you look at. Checking for these things could keep you from buying a big problem and then having to spend a lot of money to get something fixed.

Chapter 7

Planning for the Leap into Full-Time RVing

Your time is limited, so don't waste it living someone else's life.

~ Steve Jobs

You need to do a little bit of planning before you embark on the full-time RV lifestyle, but it shouldn't take forever. I know people who have spent two or three years planning and trying to decide if they should venture out and try RVing full time.

If you have two or three years before you can retire, it's OK to take that much time to do your research, but there's nothing you can do in two years that you can't do in two months—maybe with the exception of selling your house.

Don't over analyze. Finish reading this book, check out the references and links included in the book and the ones in the Other Resources chapter at the end of the book and then you will have the information you need to make your decision.

Choose this life not to escape life, but so that life doesn't escape you.

There will always be unknowns and as Yogi Berra said, "It's tough to make predictions, especially about the future."

There's one other important thing to do and that is to be sure to actually listen when you're discussing this with your spouse. Make sure it's something you both want to do. If one of you wants to do it and the other one is reluctantly going along with the idea, it may not work. On the other hand, I have seen couples where one person wasn't really excited about the idea, but after getting on the road, the reluctant one really got into it and was gung-ho.

I have had several people tell me that their plan was to do it for a year or two, but after they got into the lifestyle, they didn't want to go back to a 'normal' life. And I've seen it go the other way too.

There are lots of ways you can go about getting ready to hit the road. I know of one couple who bought their motorhome a year before they retired. They moved into it and lived in a nearby RV park for the year. This allowed them to get used to the idea. They packed and repacked their RV and made some modifications to it. This gave them time to get rid of all of their stuff. They also put their house on the market and sold it during the year. The day he retired, they literally pulled out of the RV park and hit the road.

To make your dream come true of someday living life as a full-time RVer, there are a lot of things that have to be done. Everything has to fall (or be pushed) into place to make your RV lifestyle a reality. There are so many things that you have to do or make decisions about that it's hard to even know where to start.

To make it happen, set a date

As long as you plan to live the RV life someday, it will never happen. The time will never be just perfect. The best way to make your dream a reality is to set a date.

Set a date that's realistic, but ambitious. After you set a date, mark it on your calendar, tell your family and friends. It's no longer a dream, it's a matter of fact. Consider throwing a going away party for yourselves. This will make the fact that you really are going to hit the road on your announced date more firm.

Next, start making things happen.

For most people, the biggest obstacle is getting rid of their house. Take steps to solve this problem first. Call a real estate agent and get your house on the market to sell or rent.

Don't sit idle and wait for the house to sell. You've already set a date that you're going to hit the road. Get busy taking care of the other things that must be done.

A word about selling your house—I've seen people have their houses on the market for two or three years before there was a sale. A lot of people have an unrealistic expectation about what their house is worth. Don't fall into that trap. It's worth what it will sell for now. The main reason a house doesn't sell is that the owner has set an unrealistic price. Set your price at a fair market value (or maybe a little less) and your house will sell. I've heard people say that they're going to wait for the housing market to rebound. If you really thought housing prices were going to go up 15% to 20% within the next year, wouldn't you be buying real estate like mad?

Put your house on the market, set a fair price and if it doesn't sell within a reasonable time, lower the price and keep doing this until it sells or until you decide to keep the house and rent it out. At that point, get it rented.

My neighbor had her place on the market for over a year and then finally sold it for less than she had turned down a month after it was listed. Your house is worth what it will sell for now—not what you think it's worth and not what it was worth a few years ago.

My mother and father sold their house (and a lot of the stuff inside the house) at an auction after they moved into a condo. Maybe you're not that brave, but a good auction company will get a fair price for your house. I'm not recommending that you have an auction to sell your house, but if all else fails, it's an option.

While your house is on the market, get rid of all of your stuff that you don't need—which will be almost everything. See the next chapter on how to get rid of your stuff. It's easier than you think.

If you don't have a deadline, you will never get to the end of your to-do list.

Not everything that you would like to get done has to be done before you hit the road. You are not like Lewis and Clark heading off into the wilderness for two years. You can do things while you're on the road. For example, I recommend that you get your banking set up with two banks that have branches nationwide. It would be nice if this was taken care of before you left, but you can do it while you're on the road.

You may want a better (or a lower priced) car to tow behind your motorhome. You can sell your present car and then buy something else while you're on the road.

Concentrate on taking care of the things that absolutely must to be taken care of before you leave. Remember, you have a departure date. If you didn't get your riding lawnmower sold, give it to someone. You'll be surprised how fast things happen when you really do have a firm departure date.

Once you've made the decision to try full-time RVing, don't waste time second guessing yourself. Six months or a year or two down the road you can reevaluate the situation and if being a full-time RVer isn't making you happy, you can sell your RV and buy or rent a house or condo and live wherever you wish. You're not locked permanently into your decision.

The important thing is to make a decision. It's OK to make a decision to not embark on living full time in an RV, but in my opinion, it's not OK to not make a decision.

When you're sitting in a rocking chair on the front porch of a nursing home, it's OK to say, "I thought about living full time in an RV at one time, but I decided not to do it." It's not OK to say, "I thought about living full time in an RV at one time, but I never got around to doing it."

Chapter 8

How to Get Rid of Your Stuff

If people concentrated on the really important things in life, there'd be a shortage of fishing poles.

~ Doug Larson

You *can* take it with you—but you can't take all of it.

I don't know how many times I've heard someone say, "I could never live in an RV—I have too much stuff." If this describes your thinking, remember that the stuff doesn't own you. You own the stuff.

71

People say this with the same conviction they would say that one leg is longer than the other one. They act as if they were born that way and that there is nothing they can do about it.

If you say, "I choose to have all of this stuff," then you own the situation or problem. It's easier to deal with when you look at it that way.

Your stuff can all be classified into one of four categories, A, B, C and D as described below:

Category A: Things you really are going to use and take with you in your RV—and remember a Class A motorhome can hold a lot of stuff.

Category B: These are the things that you can sell—your dining room table and chairs, the sofa you bought two years ago, your riding lawnmower. In fact, you can sell almost everything and it doesn't take long to do it.

CraigsList is a great way to sell larger items. If you price the items right and include pictures, they will usually sell within a week. If an item doesn't sell within a week, lower the price by at least a third and list it again. Be sure to list a phone number where you can be reached most of the time.

When someone is ready to buy something, if they can't get you on the phone, they will call another person selling essentially the same type of item you're offering. I have sold a lot of items using CraigsList. The system works great. You get a fair price and you get it sold fast.

For smaller items, you can use eBay. For both CraigsList and eBay, be sure to show several good quality pictures. Pictures make items sell in a hurry. With eBay, you can set a reserve price, or you can just auction it off and take what you get. After all, usually, whatever it sells for is what it's worth and that's what you wanted to do in the first place—sell the item for whatever it's worth.

I like to run an eBay auction for three days and start the bidding at $1. That gets a lot of people bidding. You can also offer a "Buy it Now" option with eBay. A lot of people don't want to wait. They want to buy your item and be done with it.

Category C: These are the things that you put in a garage sale one Saturday and then take what doesn't sell to Goodwill. This way, at the end of the day it's gone.

Basically, category C items are things that you could buy at Goodwill for almost nothing IF you ever really needed them. In this category I would list tools, old furniture, clothes, shoes, items you bought at garage sales because they were such bargains, all the extra dishes and cookware that you might use if you ever had 30 people come to visit, all of the extra towels and linens, and how about all of the things on the top shelf in the kitchen cabinets that you haven't touched in years? You probably don't even know what's up there. The list goes on and on, but get rid of these things in a hurry.

Category D: This category is for sentimental things. A few of these things you can take with you—but very few. Pictures and photo albums can all be scanned and put on a thumb drive. If you don't know how to do this, your kids or grandkids will know how or there are businesses that offer this service at a very low price.

There's grandma's sewing machine, great grandma's lamp, the afghan that Aunt Sarah made for you and the list goes on and on. Most people think that things on this list are the hardest get rid of. But in fact, these items can be the easiest to get rid of if you follow the procedure described below.

First of all decide who you want to have each of these things when you're dead and gone. Then give the items to them now. If they won't take the things now, you know what will happen to them as soon as you're gone. They will give them to Goodwill, sell them in a garage sale or just throw them away.

I know that it's hard to accept the fact that a lot of things you cherish will not even be considered worth keeping by other people when you're gone. That's just the facts. Don't blame your kids or relatives. It's not their responsibility or duty to like or value the same things you like.

Also, remember that when you give someone something, it's theirs. Be sure to tell them this. If they want to sell it in a garage sale, that's fine with you. Of course, that's probably not the way you feel, but there's no need to lay a guilt trip on them and insist that they keep the item and cherish it. Even if they do keep it for a while, it may get thrown away as soon as you're gone.

Look on the bright side. A lot of the things you will be giving people will be things they will love and really enjoy having. By giving them the items now, you will get to see them enjoy the things and you'll know the items went to the people you wanted to have them. Also, when you give sentimental things away be sure the tell them the story that goes with the item—in other words, tell them why it's sentimental. For example, Grandpa gave this vase to grandma before they were married. If you don't give the vase to someone now (along with the story), after you're gone, someone will just say, "That's an old vase she has had for a long time. I don't know where she got it."

Don't put things in storage—at least, not more than what will fit in the smallest storage unit they make. And if you do put things in a storage unit, a year from now consider getting rid of even those things. Some people have found it easier to get rid of sentimental things in a two-step process like this, but don't let it drag out into years and still have the junk in storage.

Put those things you think you just can't part with in storage for one year. At the end of a year decide if your future is full-time RVing. If so, give everything that's in storage to your kids or relatives—even grandma's sewing machine. If they don't want it, sell it. If it doesn't sell, give it to Goodwill or throw it away.

I know of one couple who put things in a storage unit and didn't even see any of the things for seven years before they finally decided to go back and empty out the storage unit.

I also know a woman who has a very large storage unit that she pays $200 a month for and she has had it for over 5 years. That's over $12,000 she has paid and I wouldn't give $200 for everything in her storage unit. Most of it's not even sentimental items—it's just things that she thinks she might need someday. Don't fall into this trap. Even $50 a month for five years is still $3,000 and $3,000 will buy a lot of stuff.

You have all of this stuff because you choose to have it. You can choose to get rid of it. You may not believe it now, but it's such a big relief when you get rid of all of the stuff that you've been hanging onto for years.

Look at it this way, if you put a big new storage building behind your house, how long do you think it would be before it would be full? We all tend to store stuff until all available space is filled.

Even with the limited storage space in my motorhome, I find from time to time that I have accumulated a lot of junk—things like the cardboard box that my backup camera came in (I thought I might want to return it sometime) and the power supply for the electric razor that quit working. I threw the razor away, but I still have the power supply. Who knows, I might need it for something sometime. I think we are all pack rats by nature, but we can change.

It will feel like a tremendous burden is lifted from your shoulders when you have gotten rid of all of the stuff you don't really need.

By the way, one thing that helps in getting rid of things is to set a date when everything has to be gone. For a storage unit that can be easy. Just say, "I'm not going to pay another month's rent. Everything has to be out by the 31st.

I know one couple who made a picture of their empty storage unit and then threw a party and invited their friends to help them celebrate the big occasion. It was a fun time.

Bottom line: Plan your party now and start getting rid of stuff.

Chapter 9

Pets Make Great Travelers If You Know a Few Tips and Secrets

Retirement is wonderful. It's doing nothing without worrying about getting caught at it.

~ Gene Perret

In all the different campgrounds I've camped in, it seems to me that over half of the campers have a pet or two.

Almost all campgrounds allow pets. Of course, there are some rules that must be followed, so make sure you and your pet both read the rules. The rules are usually straight forward, common sense rules such as—no barking, your dog must be on a leash, clean up after your pet, etc.

Things to be aware of when traveling with your pet

- Pay attention to the temperature in your RV when you're away. Don't let it get too hot or too cold.

- Have someone other than you check to make sure your dog doesn't bark when you're away. Do this for a few times until you're sure that he is not barking while you're gone.

- Check to make sure your dog or cat doesn't decide to do damage while you're away, such as chewing or scratching furniture or carpet. Some pets (especially when they're young) will tear up things when they get bored, scared or unhappy about being left. So keep a close eye on them until you know how they will act when you're away. It may be necessary to keep them in a cage while you're away.

- Make sure your animal gets plenty of exercise. It's a good way for you to get some exercise too. Since there's not as much room for your pet to run around in the RV as there is in his yard or in your home, plan on taking him for more and longer walks than you normally do. Walking your dog around the campground is a great way to meet most of your neighbors. Most cats can even be trained to walk on a leash. If you start when they are kittens, it's a lot easier. Older cats sometime have a mind of their own—who would have guessed it.

- Keep plenty of your pet's food on hand. You may not be able to find your normal brand everywhere. Changing your pet's food and then hitting the road in your RV could result in trouble for you and your pet. Don't risk it. Don't change your pet's diet unless you're not going to be traveling for a few days. Some people order their favorite brand of pet food on Amazon and have it shipped to wherever they are if it's not commonly available.

- What do you do about a vet? First of all, be sure to keep current copies of all of your pet's vaccinations. Otherwise you might end up getting duplicate and unnecessary treatments, which could be expensive and not good for your pet either. One solution is to use a national chain of vets such as Banfield Pet Hospital. They have offices all over the country. Go to their website at *BanfieldPetHospital.com* and enter the zip code where you are and you can find their closest office. Many of their offices are located in PetSmart stores. They have a centralized database and your pet's records can be brought up at any of their offices.

Bottom line: Most pets make great traveling companions. You just have to pay a little bit of attention to their special needs (and personalities).

Chapter 10

What About Being Away From Family and Friends?

Don't simply retire from something; have something to retire to.

~ Rev. Harry Emerson

Do you know who lives three houses down the street from you—in both directions? You'll likely know when you're parked in an RV campsite—even if you're only going to be there for a few days. At the very least you'll know their first names.

That's because people in campgrounds do a lot of walking (even if they don't have a dog to walk) and they always speak if you're sitting outside. If you want to talk, sit outside and you will have plenty of interesting people to talk to as they pass by. You'll find that people in campgrounds are very friendly.

Leaving your friends behind and not having a group of close friends and family nearby is probably the second hardest thing to adjust to when you first think about hitting the road. At least, it's what people think will be the second hardest. Of course, everyone agrees that getting rid of most of your stuff is the hardest thing.

For some people, it's not so much about not seeing or spending time with family and friends as it is knowing that they are just not there.

The best way to handle this is to make your travel plans so that you are back to your present home area for major events—graduations, weddings, family reunions, etc. You can coordinate your trips and take advantage of the time to see your regular doctor for your annual physical or see your regular dentist for a checkup or maybe see your regular accountant, etc.

You will meet a lot of new friends while you're traveling and maybe you don't want to say it out loud, but in many cases, your new friends will be much more interesting than your existing friends. After all, you will have a lot more in common with the new people you meet in most cases.

A new website that allows you and your new RV friends to easily stay in touch is *RVillage.com*. It's free to join and you can post your travel plans and check on the travel plans of your friends. This makes it easy to coordinate your travel plans and end up in the same campground (or at the same workamp) from time to time. Only the people you designate as friends will be able to see the travel plans you post. The website is just getting started, but there are already over 12,000 members.

You can have the best of both worlds. With the Internet, Facebook, Twitter, Skype, video chat, and email you can stay in close touch with your family and friends—maybe even more so than you did when they were close by. And since you're traveling, you will have interesting things to talk about.

Another good thing about your new traveling lifestyle is that you can plan your travel so that you swing by wherever and see people who have moved away and you haven't seen in a long time. If your family is like mine, almost any direction you travel, you can arrange to pass through towns and see family and friends along the way.

In a lot of cases, you can arrange to park in their driveways and spend the night. You won't need water or electricity because your motorhome is fully self-contained. You will be the best and most welcome guests for people to have because you won't be any trouble. They won't even have to change the sheets when you're gone.

I know in my travels I have visited cousins and they tell me that I'm the only member of the family who has been to their house or at least, the only family member who has been there in a long time. People just don't usually take the time to get in their cars and drive four hours to visit one of their cousins very often.

You may find that you will get to connect with more of your scattered family than anyone else in the clan.

Bottom line: If you're looking for an excuse not to hit the road in an RV, being away from family and friends could be a good one. But if you want to make it work, you will find that you can have a lot more friends and stay in contact with your family and your existing friends as much and maybe even more than you're doing now—it's just that you may not have as much face to face time with them.

Chapter 11

How to Find the Best Campgrounds

There's never enough time to do all the nothing you want.

~ Bill Watterson

First of all, there is no 'best' campground. It depends on what you want. For some people, what they would describe as being the best would be ones that are free. I take advantage of free camping spots a lot when traveling, but not all the time.

If all I want to do is stop and spend the night and then get up in the morning and hit the road again, a convenient and free Walmart parking lot or a truck stop or rest area that allows overnight parking is my definition of the best spot for that night.

On the other hand, there are times when I want to stay in a state park on the beach in Florida and pay the $18 to $25 a night to camp. In fact, I have already booked state park camping spaces on the east coast of Florida 10 months in advance for all of January and February and then I booked the month of March in a private campground on the gulf coast of Florida. I don't want my RV (or me) to see snow this year. I had enough of that last winter—even though I was in Florida all of January last year. I don't want the view out of the front windshield of my RV to look like it did this past February. See the picture below.

The North Carolina mountains are pretty when they're covered with snow, but I like the Florida beaches in the winter better. My old bones like warm weather.

One of the things many people enjoy about full-time RVing is selecting camping places and planning trips.

With computers and smart phones you have access to an abundance of websites, apps and information about campsites. There are databases that list just free boondocking camping spaces (boondocking will be described in detail in the next chapter). There are websites that list just state and national parks, some that list just camping places that are $10 or less, etc. Of course, there are books, too, that list campgrounds. You don't have to rely completely on computers and the Internet to decide where to camp.

One of my favorite ways to find great campgrounds is by talking with fellow campers and getting personal recommendations. Most RVers have a few favorite campgrounds that they really like and they're eager to share the information with other campers. The *RVillage.com* website that I talked about in the previous chapter is also a great way to talk to other RVers and get recommendations on which campgrounds to stay in—and which ones to avoid.

Camping in National Parks

If you're 62 or older and are a US citizen, you can purchase the America the Beautiful—National Parks and Federal Recreational Lands Pass—Senior Pass. It's $10 for a lifetime membership and it allows you free admission and discount camping (which is usually a 50% discount). This is the best $10 you can spend.

(It's $10 if you get it in person or you can get it by mail for $20.)

To find locations near you where you can get the pass in person go to:
store.usgs.gov/pass/PassIssuanceList.pdf
and to get information about ordering a pass by mail, go to:
store.usgs.gov/pass/senior.html

Half-price camping

Camping for half-price is not as good as boondocking and camping for free, but you do get water, electricity, sewer, WiFi and sometimes even free cable TV that you don't usually get in the free camping places. There are a few half-price membership plans. Below is information on the two discount camping memberships I like and use:

PassportAmerica.com—It costs $44 a year to be a member and you get a printed (and online) directory of 1,900 campgrounds that give you a 50% discount. A campsite that would normally cost you $25 a night would only cost $12.50 a night with your membership card. There are restrictions that apply. Some campgrounds have limits on how long you can stay—usually 3 to 7 days. Some don't offer the discounts on weekends and most don't allow the discounts on holidays. I'm a member because I don't have to stay many nights to make it well worth the $44 yearly membership fee.

Another discount membership service I like is *EscapeesRV.com*. It costs $60 for a one-year membership, but sometimes they have it on sale for $29 for a year. They provide discounts at a lot of campgrounds—15% at most and 50% at a few.

An App I like on my smartphone is the AllStays camp and RV app. You can get information about it at *AllStays.com/apps/camprv.htm*. You get access to a ton of travel information with this app. Be sure to check it out. You can find dump stations, overhead clearances, grades of steep mountains. You get all of this in addition to information on over 27,000 campgrounds. To download the app on your iPhone or Android device the cost is $9.99.

What others think about a campground

Below are links to two popular websites where RVers post reviews and describe their experiences at the different campgrounds.

rvparkreviews.com has been around a lot longer and has more reviews posted, but has a clunker interface and is a little harder to use.

rvparking.com is easier to use and has a mobile app. It also lets you see the profile of the person leaving the review. This allows you to read reviews of RVers who like the same things you do. I usually check them both when I'm considering a campground.

There are no really best campgrounds, but there are a lot of good and interesting ones to choose from. What you would consider to be the best would depend on your likes and dislikes. Some people like a lot of privacy like this site I stayed in at Anastasia State Park in Florida.

I couldn't see any other RVs in any direction. I couldn't see the beach either, but I could hear it and it was only a short walk to get to it. I had water and electricity, but like most state park campgrounds, I had to unhook and drive to the sewer dumping station every few days—no big deal. I liked this campground so much that I have already booked it for a couple of weeks next January.

I don't think I have ever stayed at what I would call a bad campsite. If I did stop at a site I didn't like, I think I would leave and go somewhere else the next night and if it was really bad, I wouldn't even stay the first night. That's one of the big advantages of the RV lifestyle—you're free to move on when you want to.

Three things to keep in mind are:

1. Most state and national park campgrounds don't offer discounts for longer stays. In fact, most of them limit you to a maximum stay of 14 days—and most of them don't have sewer connections. They do provide a dump station nearby.

2. Most commercial campground have discounts for longer stays. Usually you can stay for a month for about the same price as staying for two weeks.

3. Commercial campgrounds usually have RVs parked very close together and state and national parks have a lot of space between campsites.

Bottom line: Some of the features people look for when choosing a campground are these: water views, low price, pull-through spaces so they don't have to back into a space, quiet campsites away from traffic, level spaces, a good WiFi signal, and the list goes on.

Selecting camping places is one of the many things that a lot of RVers like about the RV lifestyle. There are so many interesting places to choose from.

Chapter 12

Boondocking—Camping Where There's No Campground

I'm going to retire and live off my savings. What I'll do the second day, I have no idea.

~ Author Unknown

Boondocking is the term used to describe camping or parking your RV where there are no facilities. No facilities means that there's no electricity, no water and no sewer connection.

It's a great way to save money when traveling and almost all RVers take advantage of it from time to time. RVs are completely self-contained and don't really need to be connected to the world all the time.

The lighting is all 12 volts and works for days on battery power. Having all LEDs makes the batteries last a lot longer. I changed all of my bulbs to LEDs about a year ago.

And as a back up, you have a generator to charge the RV batteries and provide 120 VAC for the microwave and coffee pot and to charge computers, cell phones, etc. You have propane for cooking, heating, and hot water. And you have holding tanks for fresh water and for shower and sink water (which is called gray water) and a holding tank for the commode water (which is called black water).

How many days you can go without connecting to the outside world mainly depends on how good you are at conserving water. If you're going to boondock much, you will need to learn how to take what's called a navy shower where you get wet, turn off the water and lather up and then turn it back on to rinse off. Also, you can't leave the water running all the time you're washing dishes. None of this is a problem if you're boondocking for only two or three days and is only a concern if you want to stay disconnected for a week or more at a time.

There are a lot of techniques that you can use to extend the time you can stay disconnected from the world. There are a lot of little techniques that add up. One such technique is to have a bucket in the shower that you can use to run water in while you're waiting for the water to get hot. Then you have a bucket of water to use to wash dishes (you can heat it on your propane stove). If you just let the water run until it gets hot, you're using up your freshwater supply and you're also filling up your gray water holding tank.

I've scheduled an 8-day boondocking trip with two dozen other RVers in a cow pasture. It's being hosted by Howard and Linda Payne. They put on several educational workshops a year. Be sure to check out their site at *rv-dreams.com.*

The purpose of the boondocking week is to have fun and learn from other more experienced boondockers. There will be some seminar type presentations and a lot of sitting around the campfire with other campers and discussing boondocking. The week will not be highly structured, but there will be some potluck suppers and some happy hour times for more socializing. I'm looking forward to it.

Some RVers who boondock for extended periods of time install solar panels so they don't have to run their generators to recharge their batteries. Solar panels are coming down in price and getting more efficient. I just checked on Amazon and found a 100 watt system that included the solar panel, controller, and wiring for $165. The controller would handle three or more panels, so you could add more solar panels later if you decided that you need more power. If you're camping in a space where you can get sun most of the day, a 100 watt system may be all you would need.

I don't do a lot of boondocking (but I may in the future). When I need to charge my coach batteries, I just push the button and crank up the generator. It needs to be run every now and then anyway. Of course, running the generator is not free.

One friend explained boondocking this way, he said, "I don't go to the grocery store unless I need groceries. I don't go to the barber shop unless I need a haircut, I don't go the to service station unless I need gas. So why should I go to an RV park and pay $30 unless I need the services they provide?"

He said, "About once a week when I need to dump the holding tanks, charge my batteries, fill up my fresh water tank and do laundry, I stop at an RV park for the night."

If I want to stop for just one night while I'm traveling, my favorite boondocking place is Walmart. They are everywhere, they're convenient and they're safe. Some of the Flying J and Pilot truck stops are good options too. (By the way, Flying J and Pilot have the same owners now.)

Here's a partial list of places you can boondock

- **Walmart parking lots:** This is the most popular place when traveling. About 90% of Walmart stores allow boondocking. Be sure to ask the manager for permission. Only stay one night—two at the very most.

- **Cracker Barrel restaurants:** They have long, pull-through parking places behind the restaurants to accommodate trucks and RVs and most stores will allow overnight parking, but be sure to get permission from the manager.

- **Movie theaters:** This is a little known boondocking place and is usually available except on the weekends. Again, ask for permission and while you're there, why not take in a movie. I'm sure the manager would appreciate it. In fact, the best way to get the manager to say, "Yes," is to say, "We're going to go to a movie and were wondering if it would be ok if we parked our RV in the back corner of your parking lot overnight?" This will get you approved almost every time. Of course, at the price of movies these days, you may not be saving much compared to staying at an RV park.

- **Truck stops:** Flying J is one of my favorites. Some truck stops have sewer dumps and most of them have a spigot where you can connect your hose and fill your freshwater tank. They have plenty of pull-through spaces. They are also safe. Be sure to fill up with gas while you're there and, of course, ask for permission to park overnight. I would ask for permission while I was parked at the gas pumps and before I filled up with gas. If they won't let you park overnight, go somewhere else to park and fill up with gas there.

- **Sam's Club**

- **Costco**

- **Lowe's**

- **KMart**

- **Rest stops:** I like the ones that have full-time security. Even if they have a sign saying no overnight parking, ask the security guard or highway patrol officer and they will usually let you stay there.

- **Federal BLM (Bureau of Land Management) land:** You will find these mainly in the West—a few are in the eastern part of the US, but not many.

- One other place to boondock is what is called **courtesy parking**. That's where you spend the night in a friend's driveway. If you stay more that one night, be sure to contribute by mowing the grass, cooking dinner for them, help with a computer problem, take their dog for a walk, etc. In other words make yourself useful and you will be a welcome guest the next time you want to stop for a night or two. And by the way, one or two nights is plenty. Don't wear out your welcome.

Rules for boondocking

Below are some rules (written and unwritten) that apply to most boondocking locations. Be sure to follow these rules. Of course, these don't all apply in BLM areas.

- Ask the manager for permission.

- Don't put your leveling jacks down.

- Don't put the slides out (maybe just a little bit).

- Don't put the awnings out.

- Don't put lawn chairs out.

- Don't pull your grill out and start cooking.

- Don't run your generator (sometimes this is ok, particularly at truck stops).

In other words, you are 'parking' and not really 'camping.' It's not actually required, but for common courtesy reasons buy things from the business while you're parked in their parking lot—things such as gas, groceries, supplies, etc. Since you're going to be buying these things anyway, why not buy from the businesses that are being nice to you?

Bottom line: Boondocking is a great way for RVers to save a lot of money. Mix some boondocking in with your stays at campgrounds and your monthly campsite expenses can be cut way down. That puts more money in the budget for gas.

Chapter 13

Pulling a Car—4 Wheels Down or a Dolly?

I don't feel old. I don't feel anything until noon and then it's time for a nap.

~ Bob Hope

For almost a year I got by without towing a car along. If you're living in a Class B or a small Class C motorhome that you can drive to the grocery store and park reasonably easy, you might could get by without a car, but for bigger Class C motorhomes and for Class A motorhomes, a car is almost a necessity.

Of course, if you're pulling a fifth-wheel or a trailer, you have your truck to run around in. Your gas mileage won't be nearly as good as with a car, but if you're not doing a lot of driving, it won't matter.

Even if you can park your RV when you go somewhere, every time you go somewhere you will have to disconnect the electricity, water and sewer and then bring the slides in, raise the jacks and lower the TV antenna—and heaven help if you forget to do one of these things. In other words it's a real pain.

Now that I've convinced you that you need a toad (RV slang for the car that's being towed), should you tow a car with all four wheels down or should you put the front tires on a dolly and tow it that way? The simple answer is that it depends on what kind of car you're going to be towing.

Many cars can't be towed with all four wheels down. A Jeep Cherokee and a Honda CRV are two of the popular cars that RVers tow four down.

My Prius can't be towed with all four wheels down and I didn't want to get rid of it (I like the 50+ mpg that it gets), so my decision was easy. I bought a dolly.

To find out if your car can be towed with all four wheels on the road (called four down or flat towing), look in the owner's manual or check with the dealer. What the manual says is very important.

Another way to find out if your car can be towed 4-down is to check at:

MotorhomeMagazine.com/download-dinghy-guides

For $1.99 each they offer a downloadable guide that shows you the MotorHome Dinghy Roundup of all manufacturer-approved flat-towable cars, trucks and SUVs for the year you select. If you want information for a different year, you have to buy another guide.

Even if your car can be towed, there may be certain things you need to do when towing it. Things like remove a fuse or run the engine for five minutes at the beginning of each day and at each fuel stop, etc. Be sure to know and follow the car manufacturer's guidelines and recommendations for towing your vehicle.

The advantages and disadvantages of towing with a dolly

- When towing with a dolly, you can tow most vehicles and there's no extra equipment or expense. Be sure to check the owner's manual for your car or check with the dealer.

- When you swap cars, you don't have to buy a new base plate.

- A dolly is less expensive than buying a tow bar for the RV and the base plate that you attach to the car to connect the tow bar to the car.

- With a tow bar you will also need a braking system that will automatically apply the brakes in the car when you're stopping. There are several types of braking systems and these systems can get expensive and all states require them.

- The disadvantage of a dolly is that a dolly takes a little longer to hook up. This is important if you're stopping and disconnecting almost every night.

- A tow dolly is wider than the car (naturally), so you have to pay attention to it.

There are several brands of tow dollies to choose from and several brands of tow bar equipment. I don't have any experience with selecting tow bar equipment, but I did research the dolly market pretty extensively.

I went with the Acme Tow Dolly. It has a built-in braking system and an all-welded construction design. It's made right outside of Greensboro, NC. I went to the factory and checked them out and watched them making dollies before I bought my dolly. They had the best price too. (about $1,300). You can get more information about their dollies at this link: *CarTowDolly.com.* I'm not associated with them in any way, I just like their product and their price. They did have good reviews on the RV discussion forums. They ship their dollies anywhere in the US or Canada for about $300.

Bottom line: You most likely will need to tow a vehicle. A tow bar, base plate and the braking system are more expensive than a dolly, but with a tow bar it's a quick and easy task to connect and disconnect your toad. From what I see on the road, this is the most popular option, but you do have to make sure that the car you plan on towing can be towed with all four wheels down.

The use of a tow dolly is another option and can be used to tow almost any car. A dolly is considerably less expensive, but it takes longer to load the car and unload it than it does to connect or disconnect a car that is using the tow bar system.

One last option is that if you're not going to be traveling much, one person can drive the RV and one can drive the car until you get to your destination. This works if you will be staying two or three months at each location.

Also, you can start with this option and then add a tow bar system or a dolly later.

Chapter 14

Getting Your Mail, Voting, Banking, Where is Your Legal Residence and Other Logistics

Everyone who does not work has a scheme that does.

~ Munder's Law

When I went to renew my driver's license, the computer kicked my address out and the woman said that I needed a physical, residential, non-business address. I had a physical mailing address through a UPS store.

The North Carolina Highway Department's computer recognized that as a business address.

I was kind of wising off and said, "I live full time in my motorhome. Do you want the physical location where I was last night or do you want to know where I will be parking tonight?" She wasn't going to get into that. She said, "I don't care what address you give me, just as long as my computer will accept it."

Even if you're full time on the road, you still have to have a legal address. Where do you get your mail? Where do you vote? Where do you pay taxes? What address is on your driver's license and the list goes on?

Every state has companies that provide mail forwarding services. They are RV friendly and they offer services to scan your mail and send you a picture of the outside of the envelope. They will forward the mail to you that you want forwarded and shred the junk mail that you don't want forwarded. These services will also open your mail and scan the inside for you if you sign up for this service—for an extra fee, of course. (Later in this chapter I will discuss more about which states to consider as your legal residence, but FL, TX and SD are the ones most RVers choose.) Note that SD used to be a popular state for RVers, but now because of the new healthcare laws, don't even consider SD unless you and your spouse are both on Medicare.

Here's a partial list of mail forwarding companies that especially cater to RVers.

Florida:

- *MyRvMail.com*—You get a discount with this service if you're a member of Passport America (which gives you a 50% discount on 1,900 campgrounds). They are located in Crestview, FL.

- *AmHomeBase.com*—American Home Base, Inc. is located in Pensacola, FL and is associated with Good Sam's.

- *SbiMailService.com*—St. Brendan's Isle, located just outside of Jacksonville, FL in Green Cove Springs, FL.

Texas:

- *EscapeesRV.com*—Escapees RV Club is located in Livingston, TX. They offer their members a lot of services in addition to a mail forwarding service. They have a network of 1,000 RV parks that offer discounts on camping for their members. You don't have to have Texas as your domicile to be a member. You can be a member and use another company in your domicile state for your mail forwarding service.

South Dakota:

- *Americas-Mailbox.com*—They're located in Rapid City, SD. They have a good reputation and many RVers like their friendly and personal service.

A Virtual Assistant

Another option that is becoming popular—especially if you're running an online business—is to hire what is called a "Virtual Assistant."

This practice became popular because people running Internet businesses could hire someone fluent in English in Romania, or India or wherever. They could hire these assistants very inexpensively to answer emails, send out surveys, write articles and manuals, make changes to websites, etc. The word "virtual" comes from the fact that they were not physically near you like a traditional assistant would be.

What you would need as an RVer is a little different. You would want someone to be your physical address, process your mail, deposit checks and perform as many other functions to help you run your business as they were capable of doing.

This person would have to be someone you know and trust, or at the very least, a person recommended by someone you know and trust.

If you have a qualified relative in the state you select as your domicile state, that might be an option.

When I was living in Costa Rica for six months, I used my previous personal secretary as a virtual assistant. (She was not working outside of her home at that time and was raising two young children). I had known and trusted her for years and she was already a signer on my business checking account. The arrangement worked out great.

The concept of a virtual assistant is just something for you to consider. I don't have a virtual assistant at this time, but if I found the right person, I might consider it. It would make me a lot more productive.

Which state should you select for your legal domicile?

The easy answer is that if you're still going to keep your house or have property where you live now and plan to spend a lot of time there, you can just keep your address in the city and state you're living in now. Get a local mail forwarding service, or ask a friend or relative to let you use their address as your legal address.

That may be the easiest way, but it may not be the best way to do it. If you're going to be having earned income, you may want to select a state that doesn't have state income tax. And there are other reasons to consider selecting a state other than where you now live.

States with no state income tax:

- Alaska

- Florida

- Nevada

- South Dakota

- Texas

- Washington

- Wyoming

- Tennessee and New Hamshire don't tax earned income, but they do tax interest and dividend income.

There are other things to consider. If you're buying a high-priced RV, you can save thousands of dollars if you register it in a state that has low or no sales tax, excise tax or personal property tax.

The three states most RVers choose
There's no one perfect state, but here are the three RV friendly states that most people choose.

Florida Because:

- There is no state income tax.

- It's convenient for RVers who plan to spend a lot of time on the East Coast, and Florida state parks give a 50% discount to Florida residents who are 65 and older. This could save you a lot of money if you plan to spend winters in Florida and want to camp in some of the Florida state parks. That would get your camping fees down to $9 to $12 a night.

- Vehicle insurance is reasonable—not the lowest, but for sure not the highest.

Texas Because:

- There is no state income tax.

- Driver's licenses can be renewed by mail.

- You can register to vote by mail.

- Vehicle registration fees are low, but you do have to get your vehicles inspected every year. (If you're out of state when your inspection expires, you have 30 days after you get back in the state to get your rig inspected.)

South Dakota Because:

- There is no state income tax.

- There is no state vehicle inspection, so you don't have to go back each year, but you do have to go back every five years and renew your driver's license in person. (You can renew your driver's license one time by mail.)

- Vehicle insurance is much lower than in most states—as much as 50% less than some states.

- There is only a 3% excise tax and no sales tax to pay. This could save you a lot if you're buying a high-priced RV.

- To get a driver's license or renew one in South Dakota, RVers are required to bring a receipt proving they spent spend a minimum of one night in a campground in the state.

- One word of caution about South Dakota, don't choose this state (or any state) if you only plan to visit there once every five years to get your driver's license renewed. If you're from an aggressive tax state like New York (and many other states are getting aggressive about taxes now), and you have only been to South Dakota once for three days in the last five years, it might be hard to convince a court that your intentions are to make South Dakota your home—and that's required when it comes to proving which state is your domicile.

- Because of the new healthcare laws, do not choose SD unless you are both on Medicare.

In addition to getting things set up in your new state, you need to make sure the state that is currently your legal residence knows that you are moving.

The more things you can do to make a clean break with your previous state the better.

Also, when selecting which state will be your domicile, keep in mind that you may be called for jury duty from time to time.

Things you can do to make it clear that you are no longer a resident of your previous state

If you sell your home and all real estate, that makes a big statement, but that's not absolutely necessary.

If you decide to rent a storage building, rent it in your new state if possible.

Get a legal address through a mail forwarding service and change your address for all of the things listed below:

A partial list of things to switch to your new legal address

- Driver's License
- Voter Registration
- Passport
- Insurance (Life, Health, RV and Auto)
- Social Security Administration
- Medicare
- IRS

- Credit Cards

- Bank Accounts and Brokerage Accounts

- Car and RV Registration

- Change your address online everywhere it's recorded—Facebook, your eBay account, any discussion forums you're on, any profiles, etc.

Since you have to declare and set up a legal address, the sooner you do it the better. So as the comedian, Larry the Cable Guy, says, "Git-R-Done."

The reason you have to go through all of these steps is that your present state would like for you to continue paying taxes to them. When there's a lot of money involved, states have brought lawsuits (and won sometimes) claiming that someone was a resident of their state.

Don't try to have it both ways.

Don't take financial advantages of having an address in your previous state—such as discounts at state parks when camping there, or lower school tuition.

In fact, if you have a child (or a grandchild that you're supporting) in a state university in your previous state, the savings for in-state tuition may outweigh all of the other advantages of being a resident of the new state, so you may not want to change your legal residence until after the child graduates.

Lawyers like to be picky with words and the word that's important to you is that you are choosing a state as your domicile. What's special about your domicile is that is where you intend to make your permanent home. It doesn't matter where you're residing right now, but where do you intend to make your home when you come to your senses and decide to settle down—just kidding about coming to your senses, but you get the point.

One last point: If your situation is anything other than straight forward or if there's a lot of money involved (such as a large amount of income or potentially large inheritance taxes, etc.), I recommend that you consult with an experienced domicile attorney.

Voting

You need to get registered to vote. You will vote in the precinct where your legal address is. In some states you can register to vote when you get your driver's license. And when elections come up, you need to vote in both local elections and in national elections. This helps establish that you are participating in activities at your new address. You can vote using an absentee ballot.

Be sure to take your name off of the voter registration list for the state you're moving from. That will be one more thing that will help establish the fact that your previous state is not your domicile state now.

Banking

As a full-time RVer my opinion is that you need accounts with at least two different unrelated banks. When passwords or debit card get lost or when there are problems of any kind with one account, having a second account could save you a lot of grief while you're getting things straightened out.

Also, when you're looking for a branch bank, if you have two banks you are a lot more likely to find one close to you. When selecting the two banking institutions, make sure they have branches in the states you plan to travel to the most. Online banks are also a good option now. Banks are all rapidly changing the services they offer.

Some features that you should look for when selecting banks include, the ability to transfer money between accounts online, the ability to make payments online, the ability to deposit checks by just making a picture of the check and sending it to them. In other words, you want a bank that is very much into online banking.

As a plan "C," I also recommend that you keep some cash hidden in your RV. There are lots of places in an

RV where you could hide a few hundred dollars and a thief couldn't find it if he had all day to look.

101 little things

Handling all of the details discussed in this chapter is not as hard as it seems. It just consists of what seems like 101 little things. Make sure you jump through all of the hoops to clearly establish your new state as your domicile. Most of the time, it's never a problem—especially, if there's not a lot of tax money involved, so don't let all of my caution scare you.

The worse thing that could happen is that you would have to pay the taxes you would have had to pay if you had not done anything. In other words, it's heads you win and tails you don't lose.

On second thought it could be worse. As one attorney explained it to me, if your previous home state could prove that you never really intended for the new state to be your domicile, you would owe not only back taxes, but also penalties and interest from when you first started saying you were a resident of the new state. This could really add up.

One other thought, if it ever came down to a court case, I think it would be a lot easier to convince a judge that when you finally stop living the RV life, you intend to live in Florida than it would be to convince him that you intend to live in South Dakota—just my thoughts.

Bottom line: Take the time to decide which state will be your legal domicile, get your mail forwarding service set up, your banking, voter registration, car and RV titles and registration taken care of and, of course, get your driver's license changed over and get your address changed everywhere it's recorded. In other words, do everything outlined and recommended in this chapter.

Nothing about all of this is hard, it's just a lot of little things that need to be done, but these things are easy to put off. Get them done.

Chapter 15

Internet Access on the Road

It is better to live rich than to die rich.

~ Samuel Johnson

In today's world, being able to connect to the Internet is almost a necessity. You may just want to send and receive a few emails or do a little more and see pictures of the grandkids or you may be running an online business. Or maybe you're in between and you want to book some future reservations from time to time and want to see pictures and videos of the RV parks you're considering.

Of course, if you're running a business online, having fast and reliable Internet connection becomes extremely important. What you want to do with the Internet will determine how important it is to have a reliable and fast connection.

Healthcare laws and technology are both changing fast

For RVers nothing changes faster than what is the best way to connect to the Internet and what is the best way to get health insurance. I have made changes to both of these topics three times while the manuscript was being proof read. Healthcare laws and technology are both changing fast, so be sure to do some research on these two topics using the resources I've linked to before you make your decisions.

When it comes to getting a good WiFi signal in RV parks, there is good news and bad news. The bad news is that many (if not most) RV parks have less than ideal (or even less than adequate) Internet connectivity regardless of what they advertise.

Most will say on their website that they have free WiFi—and they do, but there is not a strong signal all over the park in many cases and when everyone tries to get on at the same time (like in the late afternoon and early evening) it gets very slow even if there is a strong signal all over the campground.

That's the bad news. The good news is that it's getting better all the time. Two RV parks that I've been camped in recently had crews there installing more antennas and new equipment.

There are several ways to get better and more reliable Internet connections. Of course, some of them cost money and some don't. How important it is for you to have a reliable and fast Internet connection is the factor that will determine which options you should choose.

Since my business depend on the Internet, I would be dead in the water and could lose money if I lost my Internet connection for even a short period of time. Therefore, I like to have several backup plans.

Here are the backup plans I use to get on the Internet

The first and easiest way to get a better Internet connection is to **request a campsite near the clubhouse or near the WiFi antenna** when you make your reservations. This won't always get you the good spots because in many cases RVers who are renting by the month have already moved to the good spots when they became available. But it never hurts to ask and many times you will get lucky. Using this technique doesn't cost you anything.

The next free technique I use is to just bite the bullet and take my computer and go sit in or near the clubhouse and do my work there. This works fine if I'm only going to be in the park for a day or two or when I don't have much Internet work to do, but it's not a good long-term solution.

Another technique I use sometimes is to take my computer and go to a local coffee shop. I like coffee shops. I also go to a McDonald's in an emergency, but that's low on my list. I do like a McDonald's senior coffee in the mornings, so it's not all bad.

Another way I connect to the Internet is to used my Android smartphone. I use Verizon and get 2 GB of data a month for $30. That way I have Internet anywhere I have a cell phone signal. The 2 GB is plenty if I'm just checking email, but downloading pictures or watching videos will bite into the 2 GB. Watching even short video clips will really use it up in a hurry. I can buy more any month I need it. One month when I had a lot of work to do and was camping in state parks and didn't have any WiFi signal except at the clubhouse/office, I used almost 10 GB. I think that ran about $100. With the Verizon plan, I only buy extra bandwidth the months I need it.

To be able to share the Internet access of your Android phone with your computer as described above, you will need to go to *pdanet.co* and download their PdaNet+ software to your phone. There is a one time cost of

$7.95. Note that this website is a dot co and not a dot com.

There is also a version for iPhones and one for Blackberry if that's the phone you have. Going this way you don't have to pay Verizon (or another carrier) $20 a month for a tether plan. There is a free version, but pay the one time $7.95 fee and life will be a lot simpler. With PdaNet+ installed, it will turn your phone into a WiFi hotspot and you can use it to connect multiple devices to the Internet. In other words, you and your spouse can be on the Internet at the same time while using only one cell phone.

There are other ways to get connected to the Internet when you're in a weak signal area. There are signal boosters and external antennas from $25 to over $3,000 depending on how elaborate you want to go.

On May 1, 2014 the government changed all of the rules for WiFi boosters. New and better equipment is coming out all the time. My recommendation is that unless you really need this booster equipment right now, wait awhile. Better and cheaper options will soon be available. That's what I'm going to do.

When you do get ready to look for some boosters and antennas, check out *PowerfulSignal.com*. They are authorized dealers for several brands. Wilson is one brand I trust. They make some good equipment.

One device that's on the market now is the WiFi Ranger. It's a good device to extend the range for picking up a WiFi signal, but if you're in a busy campground, just getting a strong signal won't guarantee that you will get fast Internet service. The device is a little expensive, but it does work quite well. You can find more information about it at *WiFi Ranger.com.*

I'm waiting to see what new equipment comes out and for the prices to drop before I purchase more equipment.

There's another option. There was a time when a satellite dish was the way to go to get Internet while on the road, but that's not the best way to go now, unless you have one of the old plans and equipment that covers the whole US instead of just a small section like the plans they're offering now.

As an additional backup, I can get on the Internet by only using my smartphone when I'm away from my computer. It's hard to work with the little keyboard, but I can answer emails, look at websites, check on orders, etc. Of course, this eats into my monthly 2 GB of data.

Bottom line: For $30/month paid to Verizon and a one time cost of $7.95 to download the PdaNet+ software, you can have your computers connected to the Internet and have 2 GB of bandwidth anywhere you have a cell phone signal. And you don't even need a strong cell phone signal. If your Internet needs are more than just basic, the options described above are available—for a price.

There are price wars going on from time to time between the major carriers and prices are coming down. By the time you read this, you will probably be able to get a better price that what I have described. By all means, be sure to check around and do your homework when choosing a data plan.

Another thing to consider is that if there are two people traveling, one could have an AT&T account and one could have a Verizon Account. I know RVers who do this. The advantage of doing this is that in some areas, AT&T has a strong signal and Verizon doesn't and vice-versa.

The best news of all is that most campgrounds (except state parks) are upgrading their WiFi equipment and antennas. Maybe soon we will be able to take having a good WiFi signal with a fast connection for granted just like we take having plenty of hot water in the bath houses for granted. On second thought, I hope it gets better than that.

One of the problems with campground WiFi is that even if they have a strong signal all over the park, if several people get on at one time (particularly if some of them are downloading videos) things will get very slow.

One thing is for sure, campground Internet service is not nearly as fast and reliable as what you have at home, but you can probably live with it—particularly if you have some of the backup plans in place that are described in this chapter.

Chapter 16

Healthcare on the Road

Life Begins at Retirement.

~ Author Unknown

Getting healthcare when you don't really live anywhere in particular can be a little challenging.

The biggest problem is finding a plan that won't get you caught up in having to find doctors in your network. If you're old enough to be on Medicare (with or without a supplement plan), things are a lot easier.

If you go with the Affordable Care Act (also called ACA or ObamaCare), there are some hoops you will have to jump through because the problem of finding doctors gets worse by having an even smaller network of doctors.

In a nutshell, you are either old enough to receive Medicare or you're not. Here are the things to consider and look for in each category.

If you're old enough for Medicare

This is one case where it pays to be old. You're in a lot better situation to get good (and reasonably priced) healthcare while you're living the RV lifestyle and traveling around the country when you have Medicare.

First of all, if you have Medicare, you are covered in all 50 states whether you have a Medicare Supplement policy or not.

Do NOT change to a Medicare Advantage plan because these have a network of doctors and you will likely be out of the network area a lot of the time. Keep your original Medicare and then purchase one of the Medicare Supplement plans. That's what I did. Medicare and Medicare Supplement plans cover you in all 50 states.

I have the Blue Cross Plan F and it covers everything. About three years ago I had a heart valve replaced. I tell people that someone broke my heart and I had to get a new one. I ended up getting a pig valve to replace my defective heart valve. That wasn't easy because as much bacon and BBQ as I have eaten, pigs weren't eager to do me any favors.

The heart surgeon, hospital stay and all of the other expenses totaled about $150,000+. They didn't even bill me for an aspirin. My total out of pocket cost was zero.

You will need to decide which supplement plan is best for you and your health needs. Basically, the higher the deductible and co-pay, the lower the monthly premiums. If you have a lot of medical problems and go to the doctor often (or you think you will be) or if you expect to be having some surgery sometime within the next year, it would probably be better to go with a higher priced plan and if you're in good health and don't go to the doctor much and don't have anything major wrong with you, go with a lower price, higher deductible plan. It's that simple.

If you are not old enough for Medicare

If you're not old enough to receive Medicare, things get a lot more complicated when it comes to getting affordable medical care as an RVer. One option is to hurry up and get older.

On a more serious note, here are some of the things you need to consider:

- Some companies flatly don't insure full-time RVers. It's written in their policy, so this is a deal killer. Check this first and if you find this restriction, stop and look for another company.

- Next check the details of the plan's network. Will it cover you in all 50 states or just a few? If it's just a few, are these the states that you plan to be in most of the time?

- What about the out of network benefits? Some plans don't cover much when you're out of network except for emergency services. And most plans have a much higher deductible when you're out of network.

- Some plans require you to prove you are a resident of the state by showing a utility bill or other proof—avoid these plans.

- Some plans require you to live in a state for at least six months of each year—avoid these plans.

- Avoid HMO and stick with PPO plans that have a large nationwide network of providers.

- You will need to decide if you want to go with the in exchange (also called ObamaCare or ACA) or buy your own insurance out of exchange. Also, if you go with the ACA in exchange, you will need to find out if you qualify for a subsidy. Be careful when selecting an ACA plan and check the in network coverage and see if it meets your needs.

- The state you select as your domicile will determine which plans are available to you. You may decide that another state (even with higher taxes), would be an overall better choice for a domicile state based on insurance choices and prices. You also may decide that the subsidies you would receive when going with an ACA plan may not be worthwhile because of the limited area of coverage and if that's the case, you may decide that you would be better off with your own individual plan.

- Going with your own individual plan is a good option for some people. The annual deductible amounts that you have to pay out of your pocket are higher ($1,000 to $5,000 or more), but they do cover the major expenses—surgeries, etc. So if you're reasonably healthy, this may be a good option for you. In other words, you will pay for your visits to a doctor for a sore throat and the insurance will pay for medical expenses after you meet your deductible. Some of the companies that RVers have gone with include Blue Cross Blue Shield, Humana, Aetna, and Assurant. There are others and this is not a complete list.

- Look into policies that are eligible for a health savings account (HSA). In a nutshell, this allows you to put up to $3,300 into a savings account and then use that money to pay for your out of pocket health expenses. In other words, you're paying your part of your health expenses with dollars that you didn't have to pay taxes on.

- By all means, don't choose SD unless you're old enough for Medicare. SD used to be a state that a lot of RVers selected as their domicile state because of some tax advantages, but now that is no longer the case because of healthcare costs in the state.

Sources for more health insurance information

Kyle Henson is a licensed insurance agent and a fellow full-time RVer. I'm not associated with him in any way, but his website has a wealth of insurance information on it for RVers and I've heard a lot of RVers say good things about the services he provides. I highly recommend that you take a look at the information on his website to help you make your decision concerning what to do about finding affordable health insurance. Here is his website: *RVerHealthInsurance.com.* He is in the process of making some changes to the services he offers as is to be expected in the healthcare industry.

Here is a link to another website you should check out. *rverhiexchange.com*

In addition to the above information, here is a website that allows you do comparison shopping of exchange policy plans: *TheHealthSherpa.com.*

Some doctors don't take new patients and some have a waiting list. So, even if you do have insurance, getting an appointment with a doctor in a city where you have never been to a doctor before could be a problem.

Here are three ways some RVers handle the situation of getting to see a doctor

1. They make use of Emergency Medical Clinics (also called a "Doc-in-a-box") when they have a minor medical problem—sore throat, etc.

2. They use a service like *Teladoc.com* where you can place a call and a board-certified doctor will call you back (usually within about 15 minutes) and he can send a prescription to a pharmacy near you or tell you if you need a specialist, etc. You can pay the fee for this service out of your health savings account funds and some insurance policies cover this expense.

3. A third option is that CVS and some other pharmacies now have a nurse practitioner on staff part of the time, so that you can walk in and immediately they can examine you and then write a prescription for your for minor health problem or tell you that you need to see a specialist.

My personal healthcare solution

Since I'm over 65, I have Medicare and I also have a Blue Cross and Blue Shield Supplement plan. I don't have to worry about out-of-network providers.

I'm lucky that I don't get sick often. My idea is that if I have an allergy flair up or need some minor medical attention, I will go to a "doc in a box" that I talked about earlier.

For my annual physical I schedule my travels so I will be in North Carolina and will be able to see my primary care physician. I schedule my annual treadmill and heart checkup with my heart doctor during the same visit back to North Carolina.

As I mentioned earlier, about three years ago I had a heart valve replaced with a pig valve. Everything went fine and six weeks after I left the hospital I ran a 5K race. My doctor said that I could run a marathon if I wanted to. He said the rest of my body might object, but it would be fine with my heart. I decided to just run the 5K.

I did run a marathon right after I turned 60 just to prove to myself that I wasn't getting old. Of course, for the next few days after the race I was sore all over and my body reminded me that I really was getting old.

One more point. Take some proactive steps to take charge of your own health and well being. Carry a blood pressure checking device and a glucose monitoring kit with you. Keep a record of your readings. Take your vitamins, get exercise and pay attention to symptoms. Don't ignore pains and symptoms.

Bottom line: Your goal is to look at your health condition, your travel plans, your budget (and of course, your age) and then select the health insurance plan that meets your RVing lifestyle needs. It's not as complicated as it first seems. Just look at the facts, use the resources and guidelines outlined in this chapter and make your decision.

Chapter 17

Ways to Make Money Without a Computer

The trouble with retirement is that you never get a day off.

~ Abe Lemons

If you had an extra million dollars, would that make your retirement a lot more enjoyable and less stressing?

If you had a million dollars in the bank, you would be hard-pressed to draw $24,000 a year or $2,000 a month interest payments from your million in the bank.

In this chapter and the next one I'm going to show you several ways you could make $2,000 a month after you retire with little or no up-front investment. This would give you the same monthly income as having a million dollars in the bank.

I'm not going to try to cover all of the ways you could make extra money. I'm only going to cover a few ways to make money that you may not have thought about. Many of the ideas I'll present will be considered "outside the box" or non-conventional.

Even if you don't need the extra money, you may find it interesting to do some of the activities described in this chapter and in the next one just for the fun of it.

When you're thinking about living full time in your RV, having just a little bit of extra money can make life a lot more enjoyable. That's true regardless of your budget. More spendable money always gives you more options—without dipping into your nest egg.

Even $500 extra spendable income a month would allow you to live in a nicer RV or buy a lot more fuel. It would allow you to own or lease a nicer car. It would allow you to go on a cruise every few months and the list goes on and on. And of course, it would allow a couple to eat out several times a week.

After thinking about all of the things $500 extra a month would allow you to do, you might decide that you want to make $1,000 a month. After you look at the income options that follow, I think you will see that even the $2,000 a month number we talked about earlier is easily within your reach.

One thing to keep in mind is that after you find a fun way to make extra money, in most cases, you can work more or less and make more or less. You are in control.

Now I'm going to give you ideas and techniques for earning extra income and I won't be going into a lot of details on each technique. In each case, a book could be written on the technique I describe and in most cases it has. In fact, I will point you to some of these books, videos and websites.

As an added bonus, most of the money-making techniques I describe here will get you out of your RV and have you out meeting people. Some of the techniques may even allow you to get some useful exercise. At least, they will help keep you mentality and physically active.

The following information is mainly a list with a brief description of the pros and cons of each technique. Let's start with ways to make money without a computer or the Internet.

How to make extra money without a computer

There are a lot of ways to make money online with your computer and we'll talk about those techniques in the next chapter, but many people just don't want to spend their time working on a computer.

I'm sure there are several ways to make money that you have thought about, such as getting a part-time job, etc. In the following list, I'm going to give you some ideas that you probably haven't thought of. Be open minded. Don't automatically dismiss the ideas and say, "Oh, that wouldn't work for me."

Here's the list of ways to make money without your computer that you probably haven't thought of yet:

Make jewelry and sell it. There are books, YouTube videos, and workshops that will teach you how to do it. You won't get rich doing it, (on second thought, Donald Trump's daughter made $2.5 million last year selling her jewelry, so maybe you can get rich).

We're not talking about getting rich. We're talking about making $500 to $2,000 or so a month. I know one lady who travels in her RV and puts on jewelry-making workshops. She does several workshops a year and she has a waiting list of people wanting to sign up for her workshops.

In fact, for almost any technique you think about for making money, you should also consider teaching other people how to make money using that technique. You could put on workshops, seminars, give private lessons, produce DVDs, write books, etc.

When it comes to selling jewelry, there are a lot of places where you can sell your jewelry on consignment or rent space and sell it in shops. You can also sell your jewelry wholesale to other people who have booths.

Sell products at a trade show. I know people who have made $5,000 in three days at a trade show selling plans on how to build something. I have spent many weekends selling items at trade shows.

You would be surprised at what you can sell at trade shows. I have never sold a refrigerator to an Eskimo, but I have sold sand to someone in Saudi Arabia. (It was a special kind of sand for swimming pool filters that wasn't available in Saudi Arabia.)

Having a booth and selling at trade shows is profitable and best of all, it's a lot of fun. I've done it off and on for over 20 years. If you really wanted to get into it, there are trade shows every weekend that you could attend. This would allow you to do a lot of traveling while making money. Of course, doing this every week might turn into too much work. Maybe you would want to do it once a month. It's your choice.

I met a couple at a bluegrass festival. He was selling cowboy hats (and lots of other kinds of hats). His wife had a booth and she was selling gold and silver chains by the inch. She had big rolls of several different kinds and sizes of chains for necklaces. She would put fasteners on the chains for an extra fee. They lived full-time in their RV and he said they went to a festival of some kind about once a month.

I know one lady who weaves baskets. It takes her about half a day to make a big basket that she sells for $150. She told me that she goes to four craft fairs a year and she is able to sell all of the baskets she makes by going to those four shows. The best part is that she is making money doing something she loves to do.

Of course, what sells best depends on what kind of trade show it is. Jewelry, paintings, soap, DVDs, CDs, LEDs, plans to build something, and all kinds of crafts are just some examples of things that sell well at trade shows.

Ideally, you would like to have something that people can't find at Walmart or anywhere else when they get home. They have to buy it now or forever do without it. That adds the urgency factor and greatly helps sales.

You want something that's small and easy to take to the shows. People want to pay for it and put it in their bag and leave with it. Using Square or PayPal, you can process credit cards using your smart phone and the money goes right into your checking account.

A lot of RVers who want to work some and receive free camping find opportunities by checking out the websites below. Note that the work you will find at the websites listed below involves working without using your computer, but you will need a computer to check out the jobs—or have a friend check this for you if don't have a computer.

- *CoolWorks.com*

- *WorKamper.com*

Many people have told me that they select work they want to do using the above two websites. They get free camping for working a few hours a week and many of the jobs also pay a salary in addition to providing free camping. Here are some of the jobs friends have had in the last year or so:

- Tram driver

- Interpreter

- Campground host

- Working in a national park gift shop

- Pointing out eagles and other wildlife to tourists at a National Park

- Guest services and maintenance at a resort ranch

- Lighthouse keeper

- Packing boxes for Amazon during the three months before Christmas (many RVers go this route. It's hard work, but it pays $10 to $11 and hour, plus more for overtime. This is in addition to getting free camping.

- Gatekeepers at oil fields. Two RVers park their RVs at the gate and each work 12 hour shifts letting trucks in and out. It's long hours, but the pay is good for the few weeks they do this work.

- Teach music lessons in the campground and in the neighborhood—guitar, violin, banjo, etc.

- Sugar beet harvesting—very hard work, but great pay for a few weeks.

This is a list of just some of the different kinds of work that RVers have told me they have done recently.

If you have a unique skill (and most of us do), you might be surprised at how much interest there would be if you put on seminars or workshops teaching these skills.

Bottom line: Many RVers find that doing some work while they're on the road (even volunteer work) is enjoyable and, of course, making a little extra money is always welcome.

Keep in mind that you don't have to choose just one money-making endeavor. You can have multiple streams of income—that's what I do.

Chapter 18

How to Make Money With Your Computer and the Internet

The trouble with the rat race is that even if you win, you're still a rat.

~ Lily Tomlin

There has never been an easier way to make money working at home (even if your home is an RV) than to do work with your computer. Some people are just using their computer to sell their services or the items they're making at home—jewelry, paintings, baskets, etc.

Other people are using their computers to do what is called computer work—designing websites, doing graphic design work, Photoshop editing, computer programing, etc.

Don't fall for any of the work-at-home schemes you see advertised or the ones you get spam email messages about. Use the information in this chapter and do your own thing.

The many ways people are using their computers to make money amazes me. It seems like I meet people almost every week who are using their computers to make money in ways I had never thought of.

This week I talked to a mother and daughter team who where working at home and hand winding electronic pickup devices for musical instruments. They were selling the items on eBay and on Amazon and making enough to support both of them, plus pay the daughter's way through college.

One thing that a lot of people do to make money is to buy and sell items on CraigsList. Stick to items you know something about and are interested in. Some of the things people are buying and selling are musical instruments, bicycles, antiques, and the list goes on and on.

I have one friend who buys and sells Kubota tractors. This might be hard to do living in an RV, but it could be done if you were going to be in an area for a few months and you could rent a place to store the tractors.

My mother bought a vase for 50 cents at a garage sale and sold it on eBay for $75. She bought a hand-painted plate for a dime and sold it for $114.50. Of course, she knew the value of antiques and recognized a bargain when she saw it. Even in her 80s and 90s she was still strong enough and sharp enough to go to garage sales and make these deals.

One of the money-making techniques I use is that I sell items on Amazon. I do this two ways. The first way is that I go to Walmart, Toys"R"Us, Bed Bath and Beyond, Kohl's, and other retail stores and find closeout items or other deeply discounted items. I use an app on my cell phone to read the bar code and then I can immediately see what the item is selling for on Amazon.

I usually try to find items that I can get a 3 to 1 markup on or better. For example, if I see an item being offered on closeout for $20, I don't buy it unless I see that it's selling on Amazon for $60 or more. You need this much markup to make money. You will have to pay Amazon a 15% fee and you will have to pay shipping to the customer. I can make money with a little less than a 3 to 1 markup on high priced items, but not on lower priced items.

You really can find items with this kind of markup and you can do it every day. I recently bought 50 toys for

$29.95 each and sold them for $159 to $179 each. You don't find these kinds of deals every day, but they're out there. Usually, I can only get two or three items when I find them on clearance.

The other way I make money with Amazon is that I buy items from China (usually 100 to 1,000 at a time). I buy through Alibaba Express (*AliExpress.com*) or Alibaba, which is a large Chinese company.

I place my order directly with one of the thousands of Chinese companies that are associated with them. Then I give Alibaba my credit card number and they charge my account and hold the money in escrow until I receive the items that I ordered and I tell them that I'm satisfied with the delivery. Then they release the money to the supplier. I have been doing this for about a year now and have never had a problem.

Your money is tied up longer this way, but you can usually double your money in about 90 days. Of course, sometimes you make a mistake and buy an item that doesn't sell as well as you thought it would.

I bought some spatulas that I had to price at just over my cost to get them to sell. I didn't lose any money, but I didn't make anything much on that order.

I also bought 100 aprons that are not selling well. So you win some and you lose some. I try to buy items from China at a price where I can at least double my money and usually triple my money after Amazon fees.

I have ordered items from China on Monday and received them on Wednesday (I guess an airplane can only fly so slow), but it usually takes about a week to get my order.

When I buy items from China, I always negotiate a price with the shipping included in the price. That way I know exactly what I will be paying. Also, since the Chinese suppliers ship to the US all the time, I assume that they know how to get the best shipping rates.

When I have 100 or 1,000 of an item, I ship them to Amazon and use their FBA (Fulfill by Amazon) service. Amazon takes the orders, ships the merchandise and handles all of the customer service. Then they deposit money into my bank account every two weeks.

They charge more for this service. They have a formula for calculating their fees, but it comes out to about 35% instead of the flat 15% they charge when I do the shipping. By using Amazon's FBA service, I ship everything to Amazon and they store it for me. This works great for RVers.

By the way, I recommend that you only buy about 100 of an item until you test it and find out that it sells well. Be sure to negotiate when you are dealing with Chinese companies. Actually, negotiate when you are dealing with any supplier.

I have found that the Chinese suppliers will usually come down about 30% to 35% off of their stated price.

All negotiating is done by email and they are 12 hours ahead of Eastern Standard Time. So 9:00 pm to 10:00 pm EST is 9:00 am to 10:00 am their time. You will usually get a quick response if you send email messages at this time.

There are a lot of books on Amazon that go into details about how do both the Walmart and the China technique.

If you think you would enjoy making money this way, be sure to start small and learn what you're doing before you invest a lot of money.

By the way, for Chinese items, I like to find items that will sell between $15 to $50. For Walmart items, I like to find items that sell in the $40 to $300 range.

For the Walmart items, you usually have 90 days to take something back if it doesn't sell, but that's not the case with the Chinese items. With Chinese items when you accept the items, they're yours. By the way, I don't buy any items from China that plug into the wall or go into someone's mouth.

Of course, read Amazon's rules and make sure you follow them exactly or you could have your account closed and you can't just go set up another account. By all means, don't sell any counterfeit items.

When you're selling items through Amazon, you have to pay careful attention to emails and orders from customers. For example, if a customer asks a question, you have to respond within 24 hours. And when you answer the question and the customer replies with a, "Thank you," you have to answer that too. You can click a box that says, "No response required," but you can't just ignore the customers comment. This is just one example of the many Amazon rules you have to strictly follow.

After all, Amazon has plenty of sellers. They want more buyers and they sure don't want to make a customer mad. If a customer wants to return an item and gives as his reason, "I changed my mind" or "I found it cheaper," you have to take it back. It's just part of the cost of doing business. Accept it and go on.

Some people laugh at the things I sell on Amazon. I have sold toilet seats, sewing machines, blenders, gloves, tents, coffee pots, toys and the list goes on and on.

Other ways I make money with my computer and the Internet is with subscription websites. Subscription websites are kind of like magazine subscriptions. People pay a monthly fee to be a member of the site and I write and post new articles each week.

To be successful with a subscription website, you would need to select a topic that you know a lot about—and of course, a topic that people are willing to pay a monthly fee to get the information.

Here are two of my subscription websites:

- *MarketingYourRestaurant.com*
- *SearchEngineU.com*

The software I use to run these sites is MemberGate. You can find it at *MemberGate.com.*

Another way I make money by using my computer is that I have ad-supported websites. I have about 25 now. I used to have 250 websites. I put these sites up and then I don't have to do anything with them. They bring in cash month after month and year after year as people visit the sites and click on the ads—not much of course, but by having several of them the income adds up.

Some people let Amazon place ads on their websites and Amazon pays them when someone clicks on the ads. I just put eBay ads on my websites and eBay changes the list of auctions they display all the time to keep the site up to date. I don't do anything.

I received a check from eBay for $1,700 one month, but that was back before they changed their rules. They don't pay as much now. The good part is that I put these sites up several years ago and I haven't touched them since and they're still bringing in a small check every month. Actually, eBay just deposits the money into my checking account. The key is to have websites with information that people are interested in. Below is one of my eBay ad supported websites.

UsedTractorReviews.com

Writing books and producing DVDs is another way to make money with your computer. Novels outsell "How To" books by about 100 to 1, but writing novels is not my expertise. I have ten books that I have written and I'm selling them on Amazon. None of them are novels. If they were, I would be making a lot more money.

Another way to make money with your computer is to have websites where you sell physical products. Below is a link to a website where I have been selling novelty million dollar bills for over 10 years.

zMillionDollar.com

My approach is to have several streams of income. I don't depend on just one way of making money on the Internet.

One final way to make money using your computer and the Internet is to do work on *Fiverr.com*.

This is a website (like the name implies) where you charge $5 to perform a service. You might think you can't make money doing tasks for $5 each, but the key is that you offer (and usually get) extras added to your gigs. You can offer to finish the work in one day instead of three for $5 to $20 extra.

You can offer to include a different view if you're doing graphic design work and you can even list an extra option saying that you accept tips.What kind of work do people do on Fiverr? One example is the cover of this book. I paid someone $5 to design the front cover. I paid $5 extra to have the designer send me a 3D image, which took the designer almost no time at all. I paid extra for the design on the back cover for the printed version of the book.

I have written 10 books and I have used Fiverr to have most of my book covers designed.

Here are some other services you can offer on Fiverr

- Proofreading—I have used this service. You offer to proofread one chapter or a certain number of words for the basic $5 fee. I paid $70 to have this whole book proofread. Of course, you may still find some errors, but my proofreader sure caught a lot of my errors.

- Voiceovers

- Use PhotoShop to touch up-a photo

- Design a logo

- Write a testimonial

- Do a video testimonial

There are literally hundreds of categories of services you can provide. Go to *Fiverr.com* and check them out.

I bet you will find several services you can offer. While you're at the website, go through the steps and sign up to become a gig provider in one or more categories and give it a try.

I won't try to cover all of the details about how to make money using Fiverr in this book. A whole book could be written about the topic. In fact, I just did a search on Amazon and found that 261 books have been written about how to make money using Fiverr. Of course, you can learn a lot by just visiting their website at *Fiverr.com.*

One of the newest books on the topic and one of the highest rated ones is *The Fiverr Masters Class.*

You can find the book at the link below for $3.99 or just search Amazon for the title of the book.

amazon.com/dp/product/B00I07B194

Make money posting videos on YouTube

Here's one more way to make money with your computer. Post videos on YouTube and select the "Monetization" option. What this means is that YouTube will place ads on the page with your video and then pay you for ad clicks.

If you don't see this Monetization option when you upload your video, it means you have not linked your Google AdSense account to your YouTube account.

That's easy to do as long as you have used the same email address for both accounts.

YouTube will pay you about $1,000 for each 100,000 clicks which comes out to about one cent a click. It depends on the topic. I haven't done much with YouTube, but I do have one video that has had over 115,000 views. I need to get busy and put up a bunch more videos.

Some people make over a million dollars a month from their YouTube videos. It doesn't take a fancy production type of video to make money. Some of the most profitable videos are simple 3-minute videos demonstrating Disney toys.

If you want to get an idea of what topics get a lot of YouTube views, you can see the top 100 money makers on YouTube at the link below:

SocialBlade.com/youtube/top/country/US

Social Blade is a website dedicated to tracking YouTube statistics. You can use the site to track your own success with YouTube.

Unless you really hit it big, you probably won't make a lot of money from any one video, but if you continue to upload videos, you might be surprised at how much you could make every month. I have a friend who received over $4,000 in one month recently from a single video.

It doesn't take fancy, high-priced video equipment to make these videos. You will need a video camera that has an external microphone jack (and you'll need a $29 external lavalier mic.) Don't use the built-in microphone on the video camera. The sound will be terrible. You would also most likely need a tripod to hold the camera and one or two lights. That's it. If you have a good video camera built into your smartphone, you might be able to get good results with it.

CrowdSourcing—what is it and how does it work

Another way to make money on the Internet is to make use of the website *KickStarter.com*. Basically, this is a website where you list and describe a project you want to work on (write a book, produce a video or a DVD or develop a product, etc.) and then people prepay you to buy the book and pay you an extra amount for all kinds of things—such as to have their name included in the book, or pay a lot more to have one of the characters in the book named after them, etc.

I'm way oversimplifying the concept, but take a look at the website. You might even want to back a project—which means that you invest $1 or $5 or more and receive one of the items being developed or created. It's a fun and interesting concept. Check it out and take a look at some of the hundreds of projects that are listed.

One of the good things about the concept is that you get all of your money up front before you even start your project. It doesn't cost you anything to post and describe your proposed project. People generally receive about $5,000 up to hundreds of thousands of dollars to develop their projects. The concept is called CrowdFunding or CrowdSourcing. There are other crowdsourcing websites, but KickStarter is the most popular.

A friend of mine recently received over $10,000 in funds to write a book that he was going to write anyway.

Bottom line: Making money with your computer has never been easier. Because it's so easy to make money with your computer, I am now seeing more and more non-retired people living full time in their RVs and making their living with their computers. It's interesting to me to see all of the many ways people are making money with their computers.

Chapter 19

Modifying Your RV to Make it More Functional, Fun and Enjoyable

Retirement means that we can base important decisions on whims.

~ Author Unknown

You don't have to live with your RV exactly as it was when you bought it. In fact, most people don't. If you like to tinker, improve, modify or whatever you call it, you'll be in hog heaven with an RV. There's an unlimited number of things you can do to improve your RV and make it more functional, enjoyable, safer, and just plain more fun.

On one of the RV forums I referred to in an earlier chapter (*RV.net/forum*), someone asked the question, "What did you do to your Class A motorhome today?" There were over 5,000 replies (over a period of time, of course). It seemed like everyone had something to add to the discussion.

In this chapter I will list things in two categories—things I have done and things that are on my "To Do" list.

One thing I like about RV living is that there are always things you can do to your RV to make life more enjoyable, but at the same time, there are very few things that you really have to do. So, if you like to tinker, you will have plenty of projects to keep you busy and if modifying and fixing things doesn't interest you, most everything can just be left alone.

Things I have modified

I added a remote tire pressure and temperature sensing system. It consists of a sensor screwed onto each valve stem and a wireless digital readout on the dash that cycles through and displays the pressure and temperature of each tire. It also has a feature that sounds an alarm if any tire goes above or below the temperature or pressure I have set.

I know what a car feels like when a tire starts to go flat, but I don't know what an RV drives like. It's bumpy and swerving all the time anyway. And what if one of the dual tires in the back goes flat? I wouldn't know it until it caused problems with the other tire that would end up carrying all of the weight. Having a tire blowout on a RV can be dangerous and at the very least, it can cause a lot of expensive damage.

I installed a TST monitoring system. There are other brands, but I did some research and read some reviews on the RV discussion forums and went with the TST 507 system. You can find information at the link below:

tsttruck.com/product/tst-507-flow-thru

I replaced my black and white backup camera system with a color one that has a grid on the screen showing me a 3-foot, 2-foot, 1-foot and a "bam," you backed into something line superimposed on the screen.

I replaced my small TV with a large 44-inch screen HD smart TV. I had to do some modifying of the cabinet at the front of the coach, but it now works fine. The TV slides left and right so I can get into the storage bins on each side.

I had the two sofa cushions recovered. I wasn't able to match the pattern of the sofa, so I went with a solid tan color that more or less matched the original throw pillows that came with the sofa.

I added a fold-up type cutting board to the end of the kitchen cabinet. This gives me more much-needed countertop space when I raise it. You can buy the kits at most RV stores for about $40, but I just used a piece of pre-stained maple cabinet wood that I had and I bought two hinge/braces for about $2 each.

I modified the water heater to use an electric heating element. This is in addition to the propane flame that normally heats the water. I like this because when I'm at a campground, I'm using their electricity instead of my propane to heat water. I can flip a switch to use either one or both.

The kit included the heating element that screws into the hot water tank's drain hole, the thermostat to mount to the side of the tank, and all of the wiring. The cost was about $70. You can get them at most RV stores or on eBay or Amazon. The installation was easy and straightforward.

One of the most useful things I added was an **additional AC outlet** just below the kitchen countertop right beside the silverware drawer. I use it to plug in the vacuum cleaner, an electric mixer, my coffee grinder, a crock pot, and a George Foreman grill from time to time. The one AC outlet that was above the countertop always had the coffee pot and an under the cabinet light plugged into the two outlets, so if I wanted to plug in something else, I had to unplug something. And to make things worse, it was under the top cabinets facing down, so I had to lean over to see the outlet. It was hard to get a plug orientated correctly to plug anything in. In other words, it was a pain to use. I think I have appreciated this extra (and convenient) AC outlet more than any other modification I have made to my RV.

In an earlier chapter I talked about getting rid of things. One of the things I didn't get rid of was my queen-size Select Comfort air mattress. I just placed it on top of my existing queen-size mattress.

I installed a kit to add hoses to the propane system so that I could connect an external propane tank. There are two major brands of these kits. They are called, "Extend-a-stay" and "Stay-awhile." Both names are fitting because they allow you to stay in one place without having to disconnect everything and drive somewhere to fill up your propane tank. This is especially handy when you're camping in cold weather and using your propane furnace a lot. The cooking stove and the water heater don't use much propane, but the furnace can use a lot if it really gets cold. The kit also included an additional hose to allow me to run a gas grill from the propane tank on my RV. With access to 20 gallons of propane, I can cook a lot of steaks. Those little $5 canisters work fine for the grill, but they always seem to run out about the time I'm ready to turn the steaks over. And that's when you say, "I sure thought I brought another canister."

I replaced the faucet on the bathroom sink. The original one worked, but it looked old. Now I have a nice new shinny gold faucet.

I replaced the commode. The one I had was working, but the gasket was leaking and would let the water drain out of the bowl slowly. There needs to be a small amount of water in the bottom of the commode all the time to keep any smells from coming up from the holding tank. Coating the gasket with silicon grease would stop the leak for a few weeks, but then I would have to do it again. I ordered a $5 gasket and took the commode apart and somehow in the process of installing the gasket, I broke part of the flushing mechanism. Maybe it could have been fixed, but I decided to just buy a new commode for $200 that was taller and had a standard size seat on it.

I changed all of the lights in the RV to LEDs. I think there were about 30 of them. I like the looks of the LEDs and this change is a big help when I'm boondocking. The LEDs don't use much power at all.

I think that covers everything that I have actually modified on my RV. As you can see, none of these things were really necessary (or very expensive), but they were all easy to do and they make life in my motorhome more enjoyable.

Things I plan to do to my motorhome

I spent six months living in Costa Rica and one thing I learned about their lifestyle that I love is their term, "mañana."

If you remember your high school Spanish, you learned that "mañana" in Spanish means, 'tomorrow,' but the way they use it, that's not exactly what it means. When they say that they will do something mañana, what they really mean is "not today." In other words, they will get to it sometime, but not today. Below is a list of things I'm going to do mañana.

Replace the right front parking light bulb. I thought I would have to do it to pass my safety inspection this year, but I didn't. I guess the guy didn't notice.

My recliner chair has a squeak and needs oil. I only hear it at night when I'm ready to relax and lean back, but that's not a good time to find the oil can and fix the problem. I did oil a couple of places, but it looks like I didn't find the spot that was squeaking. That's one of those problems that I always say that I will take care of mañana.

The passenger side windshield wiper doesn't do a good job. I put new wiper blades on about a year ago and I haven't driven that much in the rain, so it can't be worn out. Maybe it just needs adjusting.

I plan to add a water filter. Adding a filter to the inlet to the whole motorhome would be easy, but I don't want to filter the shower water. That would mean that I would have to change the filter too often. All I want to filter is the drinking water by adding a filter under the kitchen sink. But in the confined area under the kitchen sink, it looks like it will not be an easy job. That's why I still have the water filter that I bought six months ago. I'll get to it mañana.

I plan to replace the plug on the end of the AC cord that brings power into the RV with a new one that has shiny contacts and a handle that will make it easy to unplug. I bought the replacement plug six months ago, too, and I know right where it is when I get around to this project.

I plan to add a $5 digital voltmeter to display the battery voltage. The RV has four lights on the control panel that show weak, low, medium and fully charged, but being an electrical engineer, I want a more accurate reading. Since the digital voltmeters are available on Amazon for $5 or so, why not. I'll do that mañana. I haven't even ordered that yet.

I plan to do a good wax job on my RV soon. There are detail shops that will do it for $200 to $300, but I will probably do it myself. I plan to do one section at a time. I don't want to overwork myself and try to do it all in one day. After all, I'm retired. I don't want to work too hard.

Of course, there are a dozen little things I will get to sometime. Things like sanding and painting the retractable metal steps, cleaning and organizing the eight big storage bins under the RV, etc.

The list goes on and on. I have one kitchen drawer that needs a slide replaced or at least, worked on. And of course, the automatic leveling jacks and the gears and seals for the slides need lubricated from time to time. I do spray silicon lubrication on these quite often and keep them lubricated. That's an easy job.

A lot of these projects remind me of the saying, "If a man says he'll fix something, he'll fix it. You don't have to remind him every six months."

Bottom line: As you can see, there will probably be a lot of things you will find that you can modify on your RV to make life more comfortable and enjoyable—that is if you enjoy tinkering with little projects. Likewise, none of these things have to be done if you had rather spend your time playing golf, reading or just enjoying your retirement.

As my mother said when she was in her 90s, "I've fixed enough things in my life. I don't want to fix anything else." If that describes you when you're living the RV life, you really don't have to do much. And if there is something that needs to be done, you can always say, "I'll do that mañana."

Chapter 20

How Safe Is It to Live in an RV?

A journey is best measured in friends, rather than miles.

~ Tim Cahill

In my opinion you'll be safer in your RV than you are in your stick and brick home. This is particularly true when you're in an RV park surrounded by other RVs.

Of course, you're not completely safe anywhere. The only time I've ever had my car broken into was when I was in church one Sunday night and my car was parked in the church parking lot. So things can happen anywhere. That's life.

If you think about it, there's not much someone could steal if they broke into an RV—maybe a computer or some medicine, but when there are several other RVs parked in the area, that's not where I would choose to do a break-in if I wanted to steal something.

Most muggings and break-ins are done by drug addicts or petty thieves. You won't find riff-raff and low-lifes wandering around RV parks.

The lock on an RV door is not as strong as a deadbolt on your home and it can be pried open. You can get an inexpensive security system with an alarm that will sound off and wake up the dead. You won't need to put sensors on the windows of your motorhome because if you remember to lock the windows, I don't think anyone is going to be able to open them. You will only need a sensor to detect when the door is opened.

Some people just buy the stickers that say that the RV is protected by some brand of security system. I think this gives you some level of protection.

I don't have a security system on my motorhome. I don't feel like the risk is big enough. There's not much in my motorhome that anyone could steal—my computers, my fiddle and maybe the big flat screen TV, but all of these things are covered by insurance, so I don't worry.

For my personal safety while I'm in the RV, I have two pistols handy. That's a personal choice and you may want to go a different route and maybe keep pepper spray or a stun gun handy.

Of course, keep your RV locked when you're away and at night. And don't display expensive bikes or other high-priced toys.

Have insurance and don't get too attached to your belongings. Then all you have to worry about is your own safety and the data on your computers. I contract with Carbonite at *Carbonite.com* to automatically keep all of the data on both of my computers backed up off-site—in the cloud as they call it. There are several other companies that offer this service. One of the other popular companies is *Mozy.com* and they do a good job also.

With a service like this, you are constantly protected from computer crashes and from computer theft. You could have an external hard drive and do your own backup, but my experience is that most people who plan on doing their backup this way (including me) don't get around to backing up their data often enough—if at all.

A free service you can use (if you remember to use it) is Google Drive. This is free and easier to use than an external hard drive because you don't have to connect anything. Go to *Google.com/drive* and install Google Drive on your computer, then it looks and works like any other hard drive or external drive. You can move files to this drive and Google will have them stored on their computer for you. They have just raised the free space limit from 10 GB up to 15 GB. That's a lot of space unless you're storing videos. You can get 100 GB for $1.99 a month.

Two reasons I like the Google Drive technique better than using an external hard drive for backup is that first, thieves might steal the external hard drive at the same time they steal your computer. The other problem is that I had a backup hard drive crash one time. Thank goodness it crashed at a time when my computer was working fine and I didn't lose any data.

If you just use your computer to send and receive emails, see pictures of the grandkids and maybe do a little surfing on the web, you may not want or need a computer backup service or system, but I support my lifestyle with my computer, so I don't take a chance.

To be safe when you're living in your RV, you have to use common sense and be careful. There is always the unexpected that can happen. I have opened the door of my RV and stepped out to see a black bear 10 feet away more than once, but that's common here in the North Carolina mountains.

The reason I feel safe in my RV is that the people who are in RV parks are generally honest and trustworthy people. They're not going to harm you or steal your stuff. On top of that, an RV park is not a good target for thieves—there are too many eyes and there's not a lot of valuable stuff that thieves could steal. A subdivision is a lot more lucrative place for thieves to hit.

Bottom line: Be observant, take reasonable precautions, have your stuff insured, have your computer backed up using an off-site service (if that's important to you), and then relax and don't worry. By the way, there are a lot more solo female RVers than most people realize. I have talked to several of them and they tell me that they feel much safer in their RV than they did in their stick and brick home in a subdivision.

Chapter 21

Summary

Retire from work, but not from life.

~ M. K. Soni

For the first time in a long time—maybe for the first time ever, you may be finding yourself in a situation where you have complete freedom to do whatever it is you want to do and live wherever and however you want to live.

Obviously, one of the options you are considering is living full time in an RV or you wouldn't have purchased this book. The purpose of this book is not to convince you to live full time in an RV.

The purpose of the book is to give you inside information about what the RV lifestyle is about and some idea about what it will cost, along with some pros and cons of the lifestyle.

It's great to now have the freedom to make a decision based almost entirely on what you would like to do and where and how you would enjoy living. Almost all of your life, where you have lived has been dictated to a large extent by jobs, schools, families, and let's face it—just plain habit.

Now is your chance while you are still able to enjoy life to make a decision with the main criteria being, "Where will I be the happiest and what lifestyle will I enjoy the most?"

The good part is that the lifestyle that may give you the most enjoyment won't cost an arm and leg. With one or two Social Security checks a month, maybe a small pension check, maybe a little bit of savings (or equity in a home that you could sell) and maybe earning a little bit of money doing something you really enjoy, you can live the RV lifestyle described in this book. You don't have to have all of the income sources described above to make it work.

A lot of financial advisers will do some calculations and show you how many hundreds of thousands of dollars you will need to retire, but this is based on continuing to live the expensive life you're living now—with a big house and big expenses.

Reverse the way you look at your retirement. Instead of figuring out how much money you will need to retire. Figure out how much money you will have coming in and look at what kind of lifestyle you can have on that income.

You may find that scaling your expenses and obligations back and living a totally different lifestyle might bring you a lot more enjoyment and with a lot less stress.

At least, it deserves some thought. Obviously, you're giving it some thought because you're reading this book. Take these facts, observations and inside information from someone who has "been there and done that" and picture yourself in a different lifestyle verses your present lifestyle and think about which way you would be happier.

It's easier to not make a decision and just do what you've always done, but if you end up not changing your lifestyle, let it be because you considered all of the options and came to the conclusion that living your present lifestyle is what would make you the happiest. Don't let it be because you just never got around to making a decision.

And who knows, we may meet up at an RV rally or in an RV park somewhere down the road.

How long can you be on the road driving your RV? I have an uncle who is 92 and he is still driving his

38-foot RV. He lives in Charleston, South Carolina, and has recently driven his RV to Pennsylvania and to Florida. He likes to go.

Just because you're getting older, doesn't mean that you can't be active and do fun things.

If you have questions for me, feel free to email me at *Jminchey@gmail.com* or go to my website at:

LifeRV.com to learn more about Life RV Style.

If you decide that living full time in an RV is the lifestyle for you, go for it. These could be the happiest years of your life.

Chapter 22

Other Resources

Retirement takes all the meaning out of weekends.

~ Author Unknown

This chapter has information on resources that you might find helpful and useful. Some of these links and resources have been pointed out in different parts of the book, but I included them here so they would be easy to find. There's an updated list of all these and more at **LifeRV.com/book**

If you are even remotely thinking about buying a motorhome, by all means buy the Bill Myers book, *Buying a Used Motorhome: how to get the most for your money and not get burned.* I have referenced this book earlier, but I wanted to include it in this section so it would be easy to find when you're looking for resources. This book saved me thousands of dollars and allowed me to select the motorhome that has proven to be just right for my lifestyle. At $2.99 you can't go wrong.

This book is available on Amazon. You can get the Kindle version for $2.99 or the paperback version for $14.95.

After you buy your motorhome, you will need to know how to drive it. Here is the best book I've found on driving a motorhome. It's only 46 pages long and it has a lot of pictures and drawings, so it won't take you long to read it. You can order it directly from the author at **RvBasicTraining.com** for $30

Another resource I highly recommend is the book, *All the Stuff You Need to Know about RVing*, by Ronald E. Jones and Robert G. Lowe shown below.

You can find the book on Amazon. Just search for the title. I have read many (not all) of the RV books out there and I consider this to be one of the best and most complete.

Here are some websites that have a lot of helpful information. Check them out.

Technomadia.com Chris and Cherie share a lot of useful information on their site. They have a big converted bus that they have done wonders with and made it fancy and functional. Spend some time on their website and you will soon know even more than most long-time RVers. New articles are posted every week and there are a lot of video interviews on this site that you will find interesting.

GoneWithTheWynns.com Jason and Nikki Wynn have a website with a lot of in-depth articles and interesting comments and commentary. They have a lot of articles about how they make money while they're traveling. Be sure to check out their website. They're constantly posting new and up to date information.

RV-Dreams.com Howard and Linda have a website that's full of information and personal experiences. Turn the TV off and spend a night reading and absorbing the wealth of information they have to offer. There is also a lively Discussion Forum on the site. Find a link to it in the left Nav. Panel on their site or at the link below:

RV-Dreams.activeboard.com/forum.spark?forumID=91511

InterstellarOrchard.com Becky Schade is a 30-year-old, college-educated, single female living full time in her RV. She does workamping more than she uses technology to fund her travels. On her site you can read her articles and you can learn more about what she does and her solo RVing lifestyle. She posts a couple of new articles every week and I think you will find them enlightening and interesting. Some of her articles are about her travels and some are about what she does, what she thinks and her life in general on the road as a full-time single female RVer.

Here is another website that I like. I especially like the discussion forum on this site.

RV.net/forum Note that this website has a dot net and not a dot com suffix. Their discussion group is broken into several categories—Class A, Fifth-wheels, Workamping, etc. Check out the different Discussion Groups and you will learn a lot. I check into these forums almost daily.

RVillage.com This is a great site to use to keep up with friends you've met on the road. Where are they now, where will they be next, etc.?

Below are some more websites with great information:

AllStays.com has a lot of campground and travel information. You can also get their information as an app for your iPhone, iPad, iPod or Android device at *AllStays.com/app*

Use **Yelp.com** to find recommended local services—dentist, restaurants, auto repair shops, computer repair shops, etc.

Use **RVparking.com** to see reviews and recommendations for 19,000 campgrounds. One thing I like about this site is that you get to see why people like or dislike a particular campground.

For example, one person may say that they didn't like a campground because it was near the Interstate and it was too noisy to sleep. Another person may say that, "I use a breathing machine at night and I don't hear noises."

There are thousands of good sources of information on the Internet (and of course, thousands of sites with information that's not so useful). I have tried to give you just the websites I use and the ones I think provide useful information.

About the Author

Jerry Minchey is the author of several books. He has a Bachelors degree in Electrical Engineering, an MBA from USC and an OPM degree from Harvard Business School. He worked for NASA on the Apollo moon mission and worked for many years as a computer design engineer. He has five patents.

He has owned several engineering and marketing businesses. He is semi-retired now and is the founder and editor of two Internet subscription websites: *MarketingYourRestaurant.com* and *SearchEngineU.com.*

As an engineer and a business manager, he looks at problems from both a logical standpoint as well as an economical and financial standpoint.

That's the approach he took when he analyzed the pros and cons of living full-time in an RV. He lives full-time in his motorhome and spends the summer months in the North Carolina mountains and the winter months on the Florida beaches—mainly camping in the state parks.

He also makes several side trips throughout the year to rallies, music festivals, workshops and get-togethers. He said, "Home is wherever I park it."

Index

Made in the USA
San Bernardino, CA
15 October 2016